ENEMY
OF THE
PEOPLE

The Munich Post *and the* Journalists Who Opposed Hitler

Terrence Petty

The Associated Press
200 Liberty Street
New York, NY 10281
www.ap.org

Paperback: 978-1-7338462-6-4
(Published by The Associated Press, New York)
E-book: 978-1-542042-413
(Published by Amazon Original Stories, Seattle)

Cover design by Deena Warner Design
Interior design by Kevin Callahan/BNGO Books
Project Oversight: Peter Costanzo

Visit AP Books: www.ap.org/books

Dedicated to investigative journalists
who continue to defend freedom around the world

Contents

Foreword   vii

Chapter One
The Corpse in Hitler's Apartment   1

Chapter Two
The Journalists at Altheimer Eck 19   4

Chapter Three
Hangman Peters   10

Chapter Four
Before the Fall   17

Chapter Five
Red Munich   23

Chapter Six
The Stranger from Austria   27

Gallery One   33
The Rise of the Nazi Regime   33

Chapter Seven
Hitler Exacts Revenge   42

Chapter Eight
Stab In The Back   47

Chapter Nine
Return of the Brown Menace   53

Chapter Ten
"The Solution of the Jewish Question"   59

Chapter Eleven
Vermin in the Brown House   64

Chapter Twelve
Democracy Dismembered   71

Chapter Thirteen
"Enemies of the State and of the People"   76

Gallery Two   87
People and Places   87

Chapter Fourteen
Prisoner No. 2307   95

Chapter Fifteen
Collaborators   101

Chapter Sixteen
Acts of Defiance   108

Chapter Seventeen
Liberation   115

Chapter Eighteen
The Lamb and the Wolf   120

Afterword   125

Author Endnotes   132

Selected Bibliography   138

Acknowledgments   141

About the Author   145

Foreword

Freedom of the press is not to be taken for granted. The threat is real. Journalists are being bullied and harassed in many countries, and even imprisoned and killed. The assassination of the *Washington Post*'s Jamal Khashoggi in the Saudi Arabian embassy in Istanbul is only a recent and spectacular example of the violence and censure directed toward the press by authoritarians around the world. We have been here before. The story that follows shows how the light of truth went out in Germany and across all of Europe in the 1930s and 1940s. And it shows how a handful of incredibly brave individuals at a small newspaper in Bavaria—the *Munich Post*—fought to keep that light alive.

The news media landscape in Germany after World War I was fragmented, chaotic, and biased. The press in the Weimar Republic, Germany's first democracy, was as divided as the populace during this time of political, economic, and social upheaval. Readers were drawn to publications that confirmed their own ideological leanings, not to those that challenged them. The Berlin-based *Vossische Zeitung* mirrored liberal, pro-democracy views that appealed to intellectuals and other elites. Out in the provinces, local newspapers served up news items and opinion pieces supplied by the vast media empire of Alfred Hugenberg, ultranationalist leader of the *Deutschnationale Volkspartei* (German National Peoples' Party) and an enemy of the Weimar democracy. There were also numerous newspapers owned and run by political parties, such as the Nazis' poisonous *Der Angriff* (*The Attack*) and *Völkischer Beobachter* (*People's Observer*) and the Communist Party's *Die Rote Fahne* (*Red Flag*).

Reflective of its times, the *Munich Post* (*Münchener Post* in German) did not pretend to be a neutral newspaper. It was owned by the Social Democratic Party and espoused the party's socialist ideals. The Social Democrats' principal newspaper, based in Berlin, was *Vorwärts* (*Forwards*). The Social Democrats had other papers as well.

While the *Munich Post* was not the only German newspaper to go after Hitler, its presence in the birthplace of the Nazi movement —coupled with the astonishing tenacity of its staff—put it in a unique position to break news about these rabid anti-Semites and their power-hungry leader. Journalistic standards practiced by the *Post*—but also by other newspapers—would not pass muster among today's respected practitioners of the profession. A fair number of rumors made their way onto the pages of the *Munich Post*. And while the paper justified its aggressive coverage of a huge story it broke in 1931—revelations that the leader of the Sturmabteilung (SA) paramilitary organization, Ernst Röhm, was a homosexual—by attacking the hypocrisy of the fanatically anti-gay Nazis, the homophobic-seeming tone of some of the *Post*'s reporting can be jarring to modern readers. Still, it would be a mistake to judge the *Post* by the standards of contemporary journalism. The times were vastly different, as were customs in newspaper reporting.

If the *Post*'s editors were alive today, they would no doubt defend their style of journalism thusly: There was no greater threat to German democracy in the Weimar era than Adolf Hitler. They recognized it and set out to stop him. So much of what appeared on the pages of the *Post* ultimately played out after Hitler came to power. In the grand scheme of things, the editors of the *Munich Post* got it right.

It is hard not to admire the gutsiness of this little paper, which was often a lone voice—certainly one of the loudest—in defending German democracy. It invited the wrath and fury of Hitler. Dubbed the "Munich Pestilence" and the "Poison Kitchen" by the Nazis, it provoked Der Führer. It taunted him. And although the editors were adherents of a political point of view—that of the anti-Hitler Social Democrats—they were also firm believers that the Weimar Republic's democratic principles were worth fighting for.

The editors of the *Munich Post*, Martin Gruber, Edmund Goldschagg, Erhard Auer, and Julius Zerfass, were certainly not the only journalists of the Weimar Republic who deserve to be singled out for their courage as Hitler plotted paths to power.

Young Munich-based journalist Konrad Heiden, who worked for the *Frankfurter Zeitung* (*Frankfurt Newspaper*), was also on the front lines, critically reporting on the Nazis in the early stages of Hitler's political career. Heiden wrote a book titled *A History of National Socialism* in 1932 and fled into exile after Hitler came to power a year later, eventually ending up in the United States. In 1944, Heiden used his deep knowledge of the Nazi Party to publish *Der Fuehrer*, a scathing biography of Hitler.

Another Munich-based journalist, Fritz Gerlich, made the ultimate sacrifice in his pursuit of Hitler. Editor of the newspaper

Der gerade Weg (*The Straight Path*), Gerlich was one of Hitler's fiercest critics. He was arrested after Hitler came to power and murdered in the Dachau concentration camp outside Munich.

A year before Hitler's rise to power, Carl von Ossietzky, editor of a left-wing magazine in Berlin and a staunch opponent of militarism, was sent to prison for exposing secret and illegal plans for German rearmament. Granted amnesty after seven months, he immediately resumed his work, focusing his articles on the Nazi threat to the Weimar Republic. Shortly after Hitler became chancellor, Ossietzky was arrested again and sent to a concentration camp where he endured three years of hard labor and beatings. He was transferred to a prison hospital in Berlin in 1936. That year, Ossietzky was awarded the Nobel Peace Prize but was barred from traveling to Norway to receive it. Seriously ill, he died in 1938.

It's worth noting the front-page headline that the *Munich Post*'s editors published a few days before storm troopers ransacked and shut down its offices in March 1933. Whatever the *Munich Post*'s faults, that headline should be the rallying cry of journalists around the globe whose work is threatened by those who place the accumulation and wielding of authoritarian power above the defense of citizens' rights.

The headline's defiant assertion: "We Will Not Be Intimidated."

Nazi storm troopers standing guard outside the headquarters of the *Munich Post* after shutting down the paper on March 9, 1933. (Süddeutsche Zeitung Photo)

CHAPTER ONE

The Corpse in Hitler's Apartment

Martin Gruber wiped his jowly face with a serviette after dining at a Munich restaurant and placed cash on the table. Wrapping himself in his big winter overcoat and donning his homburg hat, the *Munich Post* editor walked to the streetcar station. He was tired, having put in long hours at the newspaper on this Thursday in 1931. As the streetcar rattled through the lonely night, the 65-year-old with thinning dark hair buried his nose in a newspaper until the streetcar approached Sendlinger Kirche station, just a short distance from his apartment.

Stepping off, he glimpsed movement out of the corner of his eye. In an instant, two young men jumped him, sending him sprawling to the ground. They pummeled his head with brass knuckles, smashing his glasses. Blood streamed down Gruber's face. The two strapping young men fled into the night.

"*Hilfe!*" Gruber shouted.

A man riding by on a bicycle heard the elderly man's plea for help.

"My glasses, they are in pieces," Gruber said to the man. The passerby found the remnants of Gruber's pince-nez glasses on the ground and did what he could to place them on Gruber's face so he could see.

Battered, Gruber walked to his third-floor apartment. His daughter and wife quickly summoned a doctor. There was no doubt: This was the work of the Nazis, who had made numerous death threats against employees of the *Post*, which had long been a thorn in the party's side.

Three months earlier, the corpse of a 23-year-old brunette, her chest oozing blood, lay on the bedroom floor of an apartment on Munich's Prinzregentenplatz. A 6.35-mm revolver was at Geli Raubal's side when she was found dead. The Walther pistol, like the luxury apartment, belonged to Nazi Party leader Adolf Hitler, uncle of the deceased. Munich police quickly ruled her death a suicide. But a scrappy newspaper grew suspicious; this, of course, was the *Munich Post*.

Citing "informed sources," the newspaper reported that Hitler and Geli argued constantly over the half-niece's intention to move out of her uncle's apartment and get engaged to a man in Vienna. According to the *Post*, on September 18 there was "once again a violent quarrel" between them, and the Nazi leader left the apartment. The *Post* said what provoked Geli to shoot herself was not known, but the newspaper insinuated a cover-up by Nazi officials. The "mysterious affair," as the *Post* called it, triggered an avalanche of speculation. Much of it was salacious, suggesting, for example, that Hitler had had an illicit relationship with his half-niece and she was desperate to end it. Hitler was furious over the *Post*'s reporting. He issued a statement vehemently denying that he and his half-niece had quarreled or that he opposed her traveling to Vienna.

Did the *Post*'s reporting on Geli Raubal's death have anything to do with the assault on its editor, Martin Gruber? It's hard to say. But one thing is certain: Hitler already had more than enough reason to despise the *Munich Post*.

For about 10 years, the newspaper had done more than any other paper in Germany to expose Adolf Hitler and the Nazi Party for the criminals that they were. It published repeated warnings of catastrophes to come if Germans failed to stand against him. The assault on Gruber occurred as the *Post* was ratcheting up its anti-Hitler campaign. Just a few days later, the newspaper quoted from a top-secret Nazi document describing plans to strip Jews of German citizenship and use them as slave labor. During the weeks to come, the *Post* would reveal more Nazi secrets about nefarious plans for Jews and for Hitler's political opponents.

Secrets whispered to the newspaper by Nazi malcontents, documents leaked by party members involved in palace intrigues within the Nazi headquarters, tips that came to them from informants placed all over Germany—the *Munich Post* made use of all these sources.

Hitler employed spectacle, massive rallies and radio broadcasts to propagate Nazi lies and reduce the relevance of the news media, especially those critical of Hitler—the "lying press," as the Nazis called them. During election campaigns, he would descend from the skies in a rented airplane, like some Norse god come to deliver the truth to mortals. Hitler's election rallies were broadcast live on the radio. The hypnotic fervor stirred up by these events overshadowed normal newspaper coverage, especially among the growing masses of Germans who were becoming convinced that the Führer was their savior.

But the *Munich Post*'s staff wasn't buying it. They saw right through Hitler. They knew he had to be stopped. And they weren't about to give up, even at the risk of their own safety.

CHAPTER TWO

The Journalists at Altheimer Eck 19

As a boy in the 1870s, Martin Gruber would gaze at the Alps and imagine what lay beyond them. So many changes were happening in the world, not the least of which was Germany's growing power in the international arena after the various German kingdoms, princedoms, and duchies had been united into a single empire by Otto von Bismarck. Martin's father was also eager for his son to see the wider world and encouraged him to pursue university studies. Gruber had thought of becoming a veterinarian, but something within him made him turn to journalism. At age 24, Gruber joined the *Munich Post* in 1890, just two years after its founding, and he became editor a decade later. Gruber had a strong sense of justice. He was an advocate for the downtrodden, a champion for the humanitarian treatment of all, and a man with no use for authoritarian politics. When Gruber turned 60, the newspaper honored him with a biographical article that sang the praises of his journalistic determination to dig out the truth. "What he has achieved, in word and in deed, by stirring things up, with explanatory work, and through personal sacrifice, cannot be passed over with just a few words," said the article, published on May 27, 1926.

The other top editors of the *Munich Post*, while sharing ideals, varied greatly in their backgrounds, interests and in how their Nazi-era experiences reshaped their lives.

The chief editor of the *Munich Post*, Erhard Auer, was a man with immense clout in Bavarian and national politics. Auer was the Bavarian chairman of the Social Democrats, and for a short time he was Bavaria's interior minister. He was a highly ambitious man. Born in 1874, Auer grew up without parents. His mother, an unmarried seamstress, died when he was 2, and he became a ward of the state. Auer went to work as a farmhand at age 12. An uncle who was a delegate of the national parliament eventually brought Erhard to Munich, where he began preparing for a career in business. He was later hired as the private secretary of a leading Bavarian Social Democrat, was elected to the Bavarian Parliament in 1907, and several years later was appointed chief editor of the *Munich Post*. A broad-shouldered man with a beer belly, blue eyes, and a pointed gray beard, Auer had the skills of a wizard when it came to obtaining secrets about the Nazis. When like-minded visitors showed up at his office and asked nervously about the threat from Hitler, Auer "always began with secretive hints about the political opposition's internal difficulties," Wilhelm Hoegner, a Social Democrat who wrote occasional columns for Auer, would write later on.

Auer had so many enemies that he kept a pistol for self-defense.

Edmund Goldschagg, the *Post*'s political editor, had printer's ink in his DNA. He was born in Freiburg, where his father owned a printing business associated with the Social Democrats. The young Goldschagg studied at universities in Munich, Berlin, and Heidelberg before going into journalism in 1914. He went to work for the Social Democrats' *Volksstimme* newspaper in Chemnitz.

Goldschagg's career was interrupted by World War I. He was called up in Chemnitz and sent to the Western Front. Goldschagg was shot in the neck and shoulder while on patrol in the Vosges on October 16, 1914. The wounds were serious, but after spending the winter in a field hospital, Goldschagg returned to the front and was promoted to lieutenant in December 1915. He and about 20 men in his company were captured on September 3, 1916. Goldschagg spent three years in a French prisoner of war camp. After the war, Berlin's allure beckoned to Goldschagg. Kaiser Wilhelm II abdicated in November 1918. A new democracy — the Weimar Republic —was born. The Social Democrats, Goldschagg's party, led the new government because of their parliamentary majority. The Social Democrats created a party press service called "Domestic and Foreign Socialist Correspondence," and Goldschagg was hired on as an editor and a writer.

The Munich-based, anti-Semitic organization calling itself the National Socialist German Workers' Party caught the attention of Goldschagg, as did its leader Adolf Hitler. Monitoring the Nazis' growing appeal among Bavarians from Berlin, Goldschagg was developing insight into how dangerous Hitler could be. On November 10, 1922, one year before Hitler's failed Beer Hall Putsch in Munich, Goldschagg wrote an article with the headline "The Threat Of A Putsch From Bavarian Fascism." The gravest dangers to Germany come not from Communism, Goldschagg wrote, "but from the right . . . from the lunatic asylums of German fascism." The leader of the Munich fascists "of course denies any intentions of a putsch, but at the same time he has created a storm troop consisting of faithful followers." The Social Democrats in the Bavarian parliament had spoken to state officials "about the threat to peace and order that is mounting from the National Socialist movement," Goldschagg wrote. "The magnitude of the danger in Munich" was shown by the fact that "the Munich Social Democrats felt compelled to request state protection for the offices of the *Munich Post*." Those words, typed nearly a century ago, almost read like some precognition of Edmund Goldschagg's destiny.

Like Martin Gruber, *Munich Post* colleague Julius Zerfass had dreams that reached beyond the boundaries of his hometown. Zerfass was born 1886 in Kirn, a tannery town 290 miles north-west of Munich, on the Nahe River. His father held various jobs at the local gasworks. The family was so poor that, as boys, Julius and his brother worked at the gas plant two afternoons each week. After graduating from the local *Volksschule*, Julius began training as a gardener. He left Kirn at age 18 and traveled as a gardening assistant. With his working-class background, Zerfass felt drawn to the German labor movement, and he joined the Social Democratic Party, a champion of workers' rights.

But Zerfass, a modest man who appears in a photograph with a reflective look, his eyes downcast and faraway, had another lifelong passion: He loved to write—essays, fiction and especially poetry.

"Joyously I wander through fields,
through colorfully decorated meadows;
I walk through surreptitiously quiet woods,
Absorbing springtime everywhere.
Sap rises all around me,

There's sprouting and blooming wherever I look.
Like the wild waves of the sea,
Spring wants to spray life."

Poems like this one, about nature, appeared in his collections alongside political verses and others. He published four volumes of poems in all and was invited to read from his works by literary associations.

Zerfass's political and literary connections led him into journalism. He landed a job as the *Munich Post*'s feuilleton, or cultural, editor in 1919.

Gruber, Auer, Goldschagg and Zerfass were the top editors at the *Post*. Working for them at Altheimer Eck 19 were just a handful of journalists. It was a small operation, but an indomitable one. Of all the German newspapers that voiced criticism of the Nazis, none got under Hitler's skin the way the *Munich Post* did.

The *Post* was not the only newspaper in town. Its circulation of about 15,000 just before Hitler came to power was overshadowed by that of Munich's largest publication, the *Münchner Neueste Nachrichten* (*Munich Latest News*), with about 130,000 readers in 1932. Most of the subscribers to the *Munich Post* were Social Democrats, a minority in Bavaria. The *Münchner Neuste Nachrichten* was far more conservative and some of its staff sympathized with the radical right.

Nor was the *Post* a flashy newspaper, unlike the tabloids that were popular across the Weimar Republic. Its pages were fields of Gothic type. Photos were rare and often of bad quality. The daily paper made effective use of political cartoons, such as one showing Hitler crawling on his belly. The newspaper combined straight news coverage of major themes and events of the era with political articles that became increasingly combative and alarmed as Hitler's popularity grew.

The Führer would respond in kind. The beating of Gruber was just a preamble. Before the Nazi era passed, Goldschlagg, cast out of his profession, would risk his life to give refuge to a Jewish woman facing deportation to a death camp. And Zerfass would write in chilling verse and prose from his own experience of Dachau, the concentration camp outside Munich. One poem described killings in woods on the edge of the camp:

"Dark and cool is the silent forest.
Comrade, look how you tremble.
You sense the death that is lurking there;
You hear the banging from a gun."

CHAPTER THREE

Hangman Peters

Although the rise of Adolf Hitler energized the *Munich Post* to new levels, the newspaper had opposed injustice and exposed wrongdoing since its founding. A story from decades earlier and far away—originating in the interior of eastern Africa, where the Germans had established a colony—shows the paper's determination to challenge a powerful establishment and report the truth.

One day in 1891, at the Germans' colonial station on the slopes of Mount Kilimanjaro, Dr. Carl Peters was calmly finishing his meal as a teenage servant, a native boy named Mabruk, was being hanged outside the tent. The rope broke, but no matter. The executioners found another to finish the job. Peters had the boy executed for breaking into the hut where Peters kept his black concubines and having sex with one of them, named Jagodjo. Three months later, Peters had Jagodjo hanged as well after she tried twice to flee.

Six years later, Peters faced a trial in Germany for the deaths of Mabruk and Jagodjo. Peters insisted that his position had given him the power of life or death over Africans. He was convicted and stripped of his authority as a high commissioner and of his government pension. But Peters had many supporters in Germany who felt that as a superior race, whites had a God-given right to treat blacks however they wanted —an attitude that later made Peters a hero among the Nazis.

The *Munich Post* did not share that view. In 1906, the newspaper ran a series of articles questioning Peters' sanity, accusing him of cowardice and of committing a "sex murder." Sitting at the defendants' table in a Munich courtroom libel trial was Martin Gruber, as the editor responsible for publication of the articles. Despite Peters' acknowledgment of the hangings and despite lying to his superiors about the circumstances, the court found that the *Post* had libeled him and ordered Gruber to pay a fine. The trial was a sensation. And it marked the first time an international spotlight was shone on the *Munich Post* and its championing of what would now be widely seen as a just and humanitarian cause. It would not be the last time.

Although the "Peters Scandal" peaked two decades before the founding of the Nazi Party, the saga is worth recounting because of the *Munich Post*'s role in it, and because of the veneration of Peters in Nazi Germany, where he was viewed as something of an Aryan demigod.

On a June day in 1891, Carl Peters arrived in Tanga, a port city on the Indian Ocean and the headquarters for Germany's East Africa colony. Peters had an appointment with the colonial governor, Baron Julius von Soden.

Peters was no newcomer to Africa. In 1884, he and two other Germans journeyed into the interior of eastern Africa. The expedition was carrying what Peters figured was needed to persuade chiefs to cede their lands to the Germans: gifts, grog, and guns.

The Germans would fire their rifles into the air, ply chiefs with the alcohol, negotiate, and then present the chiefs with documents bearing German words. Although the chiefs could not read the words, they signed the documents anyway, with three crosses instead of signatures. In return for turning over lands to the foreign men, the chiefs were told the document guaranteed they would be protected from attack.

The Germans returned to the coast five weeks later, bearing twelve so-called "protection treaties." The 28-year-old Peters considered this a great conquest, a fortuitous start to what he envisioned as "increased power and life enrichment for the stronger, better race" at the expense of the "weaker and inferior" natives.

The following year, Kaiser Wilhelm I granted Peters' request to issue a proclamation placing about 140,000 square kilometers (about 87,000 square miles) of African territory under German protection. In 1891, the vast expanse of territory officially became a colony when it was placed under the administrative authority of the German government.

The colony encompassed present-day Burundi, Rwanda, the continental portion of Tanzania, and part of Mozambique. Kilimanjaro, at 19,341 feet Africa's tallest summit, was included. Native tribes lived in small settlements on the slopes of Kilimanjaro. Peters was appointed imperial high commissioner for the German station on Kilimanjaro. Among Soden's instructions to Peters was that he avoid going to war with the natives, as recounted in a book by Arne Perras, *Carl Peters and German Imperialism 1856-1918: A Political Biography*.

But on August 30, 1891, Peters set out on a march to a settlement of the Warombo tribe following the murder of two messengers the commissioner had sent there. Peters and his troops burned houses and battled Warombo warriors. Peters launched another attack on the Warombo a month later. Warombo warriors counter-attacked but they were no match for Peters' firepower. Peters wrote that his troops had killed 124 Africans that day. But it wasn't such conflict that led to one of the biggest scandals in Germany's colonial history. It was the treatment of Mabruk and Jagodjo.

Sneaking one night into the hut where the German men kept their African concubines, Peters' boy servant stole some cigars and had sex with Jagodjo, considered by Peters to be his personal property and wife under African law. A kangaroo court consisting of Peters and two of his men sentenced Mabruk to be executed.

A few weeks later, Jagodjo and some other native women disappeared from the compound. Peters tracked them down to a Rombo chief's fort. The Germans torched the chief's huts and recaptured the women. Sitting in a bamboo chair, Peters watched as the women were whipped. Peters warned them they'd be executed if they tried to flee again. This didn't deter Jagodjo, who once again ran off. When she was returned, the kangaroo court sentenced her to death as well.

European missionaries working in the area complained about Peters' brutality toward natives. His superiors called him back to the coast and later to Berlin.

Peters' plans to go into politics came to a halt when the Reichstag convened in the spring of 1896 to pass a budget for Germany's colonial operations. Opponents and skeptics of Germany's expansionism used the parliamentary session to relate terrifying stories about colonial atrocities.

In a speech, August Bebel, leader of the Social Democrats, told the assembly that Peters had confessed to a British bishop that he had Jagodjo hanged but was justified because he had been married to her according to native customs and she had committed adultery. In a letter read to the parliamentary deputies, Peters defended himself, claiming Mubrak was hanged for burglary and Jagodja for espionage. Most shocking to many Reichstag deputies was not the murders but the thought that Peters had lived according to savage customs instead of as a civilized Christian.

There was a great deal of empathy for Peters, whose supporters argued he had no choice but to use force to maintain order. They were sharply at odds with the German left, especially the Social Democrats. Their main newspaper, *Vorwärts*, sister paper of the *Munich Post*, wrote that Peters "shot dead African Negroes as if they were sparrows and with pleasure lynched Negro girls after they satisfied his lust."

Peters was brought to trial before the Disciplinary Court for German Protectorates in April 1897. He was convicted for the executions and for filing false reports on the incident and he was booted from the colonial service.

Peters moved to London, and from there organized expeditions to Africa to search for gold. He caught the attention of people in his homeland with an autobiography about his Africa exploits. He received invitations in Germany to give talks about his African adventures, and in 1906, he received back-to-back requests to give lectures in Munich. This is where he ran afoul of the *Munich Post*.

Several hundred people gathered inside the elegant Vier Jahreszeiten hotel to hear Peters on December 14, where he said Germans were soft because they were not competing aggressively with Britain for world power. The next day, Peters spoke at the Bürgerbräukeller beer hall, with about 3,000 in attendance. He demanded that Africans be put to work with a "hoe and a pick."

This did not escape the attention of *Post* editor Martin Gruber. In three articles about the speeches, the paper referred to him as "hangman Peters," said he was mentally ill, wrote of his "mad stammering," and denounced his "jolly hunting for Negroes." Peters was a "cowardly murderer," the newspaper said, and the hangings on Kilimanjaro were a "ruthlessly ingenious sex murder."

Peters filed a libel lawsuit against Gruber. Working against the *Munich Post* was the growing influence of racist right-wingers and a militancy that spurred German enthusiasm for going to war with Britain, France and their allies in 1914 and would set the stage for Hitler. The Munich judge ruled that the *Post* had defamed Peters and ordered Gruber to pay a fine, plus the costs of the trial. Peters' supporters had already begun campaigns to clear his name. In 1914, four years before Peters died at age 62, Kaiser Wilhelm II ordered the restoration of his pension.

The attacks on Peters in the pages of the *Munich Post* would hardly be acceptable under today's standards of journalism. But the libel trial serves as a vivid illustration of the newspaper's zeal to enter a fight not just as a mouthpiece for the Social Democrats but, more importantly, as a determined voice for humanitarian principles — even when these were anathema to broad swaths of the German populace.

Gruber would return to the courtroom again and again to defend the *Munich Post*, often from accusations of slander brought by authoritarian personalities, especially after the founding of the National Socialist German Workers' Party and Hitler's rise to become its leader.

Gruber was the bulldog of the *Munich Post*. As the newspaper put it in the May 1926 article marking his 60th birthday: "Gruber loved a good court fight."

In March 1983, a journalist who worked for the *Munich Post* during the Weimar era —Wilhelm Lukas Kristl —wrote an article for the *Süddeutsche Zeitung* newspaper about its forerunner, the *Munich Post*.

During its life span of nearly five decades, Kristl wrote, "the *Munich Post* took on the role of a public prosecutor —even in times that were damned difficult."

There was no one at the *Post* who was a greater embodiment of that spirit than Martin Gruber.

As for Hangman Peters, during the Third Reich the deceased colonialist rose into the Nazi Valhalla of Teutons worthy of being idolized. He was fully rehabilitated by Hitler in 1937. Numerous books were written about his adventures. A 1940 movie glorified his time as commissioner on Kilimanjaro. Streets were even named after him. German communities have been replacing those street signs over the years, but they are still to be found in some places.

CHAPTER FOUR

Before the Fall

On his way out the door of the small Munich hotel where he was living along with other bohemians in 1913, young Julius Zerfass stopped briefly in the parlor to say good night to the owner, a former seaman known to the denizens of the establishment as "Papa Führmann." Then, sauntering down the streets and alleyways, Zerfass anticipated another night of elbow-rubbing with painters, poets, novelists, sculptors, essayists, composers, and others drawn to the culture-rich hive of Schwabing, his neighborhood just north of Munich's Old Town.

One of his favorite haunts was the Torggelstube wine bar. There, Zerfass might watch internationally known dramatists Frank Wedekind and Max Halbe quarreling over the merits of a new play. "But by midnight, merry with wine, they were able to make up," Zerfass reminisced years later in an essay.

Another favorite hangout was the Café Stefanie. On any given afternoon, among the artists, tale-tellers and free-thinkers you'd see there were Viennese satirist Alexander Roda Roda — resplendent in his red vest and monocle — and Erich Mühsam, a cabaret performer, essayist and anarchist from the northern port city

Lübeck. The rotund Roda Roda and the wild-eyed Mühsam sat at the same marble table each afternoon, immersed in discussions about art, life and politics.

At the Café Stefanie, at the Torggelstube, at a pub called Alter Simpl, and other Schwabing watering holes, Zerfass might encounter the novelist brothers Thomas and Heinrich Mann, poets such as Rainer Maria Rilke and Stefan George, the theatrical producer Erwin Piscator, and the abstract painters Paul Klee and Wassily Kandinsky.

Before it became a capital of evil, a den of Nazi pestilence, Munich was Germany's capital of culture. Creative creatures from across Europe came here to live, to work and to play, specifically in the Schwabing neighborhood. Munich rivaled Paris in its bohemian appeal, and certainly outshone Berlin. Ironically, this magnet for innovators developed in Bavaria, where natives typically clung stubbornly to their Roman Catholicism, to their monarchy, to their folk ways, in short, to their southernness. Still, though differences of opinion would arise between the locals, wearing their dirndl skirts and lederhosen, and the Schwabingers, as the creative outsiders were called, for the most part, a peaceful co-existence prevailed.

Julius Zerfass came here to pursue the life of a writer — of a poet, to be precise. His soul found a home in Munich. To read essays he wrote years later, after the Third Reich's demise, is to absorb the sadness, the spiritual ache that he felt for the remainder of his life over what became of Munich and all of Germany.

Schwabing, Mühsam once humorously wrote, was a draw not just for artists, but also for "loafers, philosophers, religious founders, sexual moralists, psychoanalysts, musicians, architects, craftswomen, runaway girls of good family, eternal students, the industrious and the idle, those with a lust for life and those who were world-weary, those who wore their hair unkempt, and those who parted it neatly."

Plays, cabaret, comedy acts, art exhibits, music, dancing — these were the trademarks of Schwabing, as were serious drinking and the practice of free love among its creative residents. One of its most notorious inhabitants, Countess Franziska zu Reventlow, aka the "Queen of Schwabing," worked as a part-time prostitute because she was unable to sell her paintings.

On the other hand, as Zerfass wrote in an essay titled "Schwabing:" "If a painter sold something, he was able to eat well, and cheaply, at one of the many Spanish or Italian restaurants where you could order spaghetti for 40 pfennigs." And hard-up artists unable to sell a painting were able to get credit at the neighborhood's cafes, bars and markets.

Anarchists, communists, the promiscuous, dabblers in the occult, and mangy-looking artists looking for handouts were surely not what three generations of Bavarian kings had in mind as they tapped the ample coffers of the Wittelsbach dynasty to transform the capital into an eminently winsome city over the course of two centuries — with elegant boulevards, Italian Renaissance-style public buildings and magnificent art museums.

The first wave of creative outsiders moved to Munich in the mid-1800s. They included the Norwegian playwright Henrik Ibsen, who called Munich a "genius among cities." A lively cultural scene had taken root in Munich in the late 1800s, but it was still a fairly staid one. An avant-garde group calling itself the Modern Life Society was determined to change that. At lectures organized by the society, speakers skewered the Catholic church,

Bavarian conservatism and a local poets' group seen by the society as stuck in the past.

As a poet, a socialist, and an outsider, Zerfass felt right at home in free-wheeling, free-living, free-thinking Schwabing. He had trained as a gardener but was forced to abandon that trade because of an accident with a gardening knife that left him with a permanent limp. He had already been writing poems and was having some literary success.

Zerfass stayed at the Pension Führmann, where the easy-going proprietor embraced his free-spirited guests. If one of Papa Führmann's residents couldn't afford to pay his bill for the month, he'd work it out with them. And if a resident disappeared into his or her room with someone of the opposite sex for an hour or two, that was OK as well. Freedom of expression was encouraged at Pension Führmann, whatever form that might take.

"He loved his little hotel," Zerfass reminisced in his "Schwabing" essay. "And his guests were allowed to be as crazy as they liked; he never got more than his fill of it."

The rooms may have been small at the Pension Führmann but they were inexpensive, as were the tasty meals cooked up by Papa's wife, a Dutchwoman. The Pension Führmann was so popular that spillover living space had to be created in a neighboring apartment house. The hotel had three dining rooms. One of these was called the "Balkan," because that's where artists from Eastern Europe, a clique unto themselves, chose to dine. The main dining room had a piano. After Sunday dinners, the table was shoved aside to create space for dancing as someone played tunes on the piano. Papa Führmann presided over all the meals. As a man of the sea, he liked to tell tales, many of them ribald, adding even more spice to conversations that were already generously seasoned with Schwabinger wit.

Papa Führmann always paid homage to the start of the bock beer season by taking his hotel guests on a pilgrimage to a beer garden near Dachau, Zerfass wrote. "The host opened the barn floor for dancing. This trip into the countryside developed into a pure Bruegel-like carnival, a festival of the nations, a wild fraternization," Zerfass remembered.

Zerfass described a night of Schwabinger partying during Fasching, the German Carnival season, at the Pension Führmann. There was dancing, drinking and eating into the early morning hours.

"In one of the small dining rooms, a bar offered a generous selection of snacks and drinks. A record player and a piano player took turns supplying dance music," Zerfass wrote. Costumes worn by the revelers were a "triumph of improvisation, made from batiste, wall hangings, carpets, conquests of all types and tradition in Schwabing style—exquisite and unique."

At about 4 a.m., the party broke up. Some revelers returned to their rooms. Others set out on what had become a tradition among Schwabingers: walking to the "Donisl," a pub that opened its doors at 5 a.m. for night-owls. For those looking for the hair of the dog after a night of carousing, beer was available. For those looking for a snack, the Weisswurst sausage was a favorite. Or you could get a cup of strong coffee. This is the way Zerfass describes the Schwabingers in the process of sobering up at the Donisl: "There they sat, quaking in a sour atmosphere of beer and tobacco smoke with the remaining scraps of their wit, living incarnates of a hangover."

The route back to Schwabing was through Munich's English Garden, an idyllic, magnificent expanse of open green meadows, woods and murmuring streams. As the tired partiers made their way through that park on that Fasching morning, before there was even a glimmer of sunrise, they listened as "blackbirds gave their spring concert rehearsal," Zerfass wrote. "It was beautiful, beautiful like it has never been since."

The magic of Schwabing came to an end with the onset of World War I. A number of the artists were sent off to war. Foreigners, especially those whose countries were now at war with Germany, returned to their homelands. Some of the Schwabingers, like Franz Marc, died in battle. Militancy and nationalistic sentiments spread across Germany, even infiltrating the little protected island of idealism known as Schwabing.

"Old Munich died with the start of the First World War, and with it died the Montmartre-like spirit" of the beloved neighborhood, Zerfass wrote.

He was not among those swept up by jingoism and nationalist sentiments. Nor was he among those who went off to war. He was spared having to serve by the stab wound to his leg in his earlier life as a gardener. He continued writing poetry, sometimes letting his pacifist side show. He married a local woman, Anna Ziener, on June 14, 1916. In a poem dedicated to her, Zerfass wrote:

"There is one thing that belongs not to the king
Something that will never be his . . .
It is my heart, my true treasure."

CHAPTER FIVE

Red Munich

On Nov. 7, 1918, more than 80,000 people massed on Munich's Theresienwiese, a vast park that each year is the site of the Oktoberfest. They did not come to quaff beer. They came to demand an end to the war. They were tired of the endless stream of mutilated soldiers arriving from the front. Tired of food shortages. Tired of sacrificing for a war Germans across the country were ceasing to support. And so, this noisy, unhappy throng was all ears when Kurt Eisner stood up to address them.

Eisner, a drama critic and transplant from Berlin, was a regular at Schwabing's bars and cafes. He was also a leading member of the Independent Social Democrats — a radical offshoot of the mainstream Majority Social Democrats. During the previous three months, Eisner had organized workers' strikes against Germany's participation in World War I. Similar strikes were occurring across Germany.

"Munich shall arise within the coming days," Eisner shouted at the crowd. But it occurred that very day. Led by Eisner, an army of protesters marched out of the Theresienwiese, picking up more and more supporters along the way and taking over military posts. Later that day, Eisner was elected head of a provisional government by workers and soldiers, and he proclaimed the creation of the Bavarian Republic. Bavaria's monarch, King Ludwig III, and his wife Queen Maria Therese fled from their grand palace in the center of Munich, hopping into a chauffeur-driven car that took them to Austria.

Ludwig was the first monarch to get booted during revolts that swept across Germany in the closing days of World War I. Two days after Ludwig's ouster, on November 9, Kaiser Wilhelm II himself abdicated. World War I ended two days later. Germany was proclaimed a democratic republic, to be governed by a parliamentary system. But chaos and violence persisted across Germany. And nowhere was it worse than in Bavaria.

Though Eisner put together a coalition government that included the mainstream Majority Social Democrats, unrest continued because of food shortages, inflation and disagreements over the future course of Bavaria. Exacerbating the turmoil was the growing influence of far-right "völkisch" groups, especially in the Bavarian countryside. Among these was the anti-Semitic Thule Society, whose numbers included men who later became leading members of the Nazi Party.

Fear of communism had swept across Germany after the recent Bolshevik Revolution in Russia, and because of the worker revolts in Germany. Many Bavarians feared Eisner was taking them down the same path. So, when elections were held on Jan. 12, 1919, they went badly for him. The conservative Bavarian People's Party was the biggest winner, capturing 35 percent of the vote, followed by 33 percent for the Majority Social Democratic Party. Eisner's Independent Social Democrats won only 3 percent, and just 3 out of 180 seats in the state Parliament that were up for election.

The political chaos only deepened then. Before Eisner could officially resign his post, he was assassinated just after walking out of his office, his farewell speech in his hand. He was shot down in the street by Count Anton Arco auf Valley, an Austrian-born anti-Semite who had been rejected for membership in the Thule Society because his mother was Jewish.

Leftist radicals in Munich—a number of them regulars at Schwabing's cafes and beer halls—launched a revolt that sent Eisner's successor, Johannes Hoffmann, and his cabinet fleeing north to the city of Bamberg. The radicals, led by Eugen Levine, a Russian-born Jew, declared Bavaria was now a Soviet republic, in German, a *Räterepublik*. Opponents dubbed it the "Schwabing Soviet." The new leaders ordered the nationalization of banks and the collectivization of farms, decided that students would take over the running of universities, and revolutionary tribunals would be created to track down counter-revolutionaries.

Hoffmann assembled an assault force whose fighters included members of militias called Freikorps, or Free Corps. They were veterans of World War I, and many of them were nationalist anti-Semites. One of the units, the Bavarian Free Corps, had as its second in command Ernst Röhm, the man who later became head of the Nazis' Sturmabteilung. The Bavarian Free Corps was led by Franz Ritter von Epp, who in March 1933 was hand-picked by Hitler to be the Nazis' leader of Bavaria.

Freikorps troops attacked Red militiamen on April 30 at Starnberg and Dachau, killing 20 medical orderlies and eight communist soldiers. The Red forces shot hostages in revenge. On May 1, Hoffmann's forces entered Munich and encountered little opposition. The fiercest fighting was on Karlsplatz, where flamethrowers were used to burn out Red resisters. Communist fighters held out at the train station during the night, but their cause was already a lost one. Freikorps troops went on a killing spree to wipe out all vestiges of resistance. Militiamen committed to communism lay dead on the streets. Their surviving comrades were chased down Munich's alleys.

Thirty-three-year-old Julius Zerfass was hired by the *Munich Post* during this upheaval. He recalled those dangerous times in an essay, "My Debut As An Editor," written in the 1950s.

He recounted death threats against the *Post* by hot-headed radicals. He recalled an angry Red soldier showing up at the newspaper office and demanding a correction for an article that had disparaged him. The *Post* walked an editorial tightrope by trying to publish frank reports about the Reds' chaotic and incompetent rule of Munich without running the risk of getting raided and shut down.

"It was our journalistic duty to give voice to democratic socialism in the face of a dictatorship by a minority," Zerfass wrote in his essay, meaning the communists who seized power.

Like others who worked for the *Munich Post*, Zerfass had no more use for communists than they had for their ideological opposites on the extreme right.

"My Debut As An Editor" ends with a melancholy reflection on the tragic series of events that connect the German revolts of 1918 and 1919, Hitler's failed Beer Hall Putsch in 1923, political murders by Nazis, Germans' embrace of Hitler, and the Nazis' violent takeover of his beloved *Munich Post* on March 9, 1933.

"At the end" of this cavalcade of sorrows, Zerfass wrote, "was catastrophe for German democracy, which also sealed the fate of our proud newspaper."

CHAPTER SIX

The Stranger from Austria

Lofty twin domes rise from Munich's Gothic Frauenkirche cathedral, and it is easy to imagine their shadow falling, one sticky summer day in 1913, on a shabbily-dressed 24-year-old with spooky blue eyes and a hank of limp hair drooping over his forehead and on his collection of watercolor paintings. The thin young man with the Austrian accent sold his landscapes wherever he could, or tried. Too often, though, people walked right past, ignoring the works and their creator, the young Adolf Hitler.

At 11:00 a.m. each day, the chimes of the glockenspiel on New City Hall rang out. The 32 life-size figures on the glockenspiel's carousel stirred into motion to reenact the marriage ceremony of Duke Wilhelm V to Renata of Lorraine. A mechanical golden bird at the top chirped three times, signaling the end of the show.

Picture a disappointed Hitler picking up his things and walking away, heading to a beer hall where perhaps he could make a sale. At the end of the day, he would return to the room he rented above a tailor's shop in the Schwabing district. He didn't seek out the company of any of the other artists, even though Schwabing was famously filled with them. There were too many Jews among them, too many communists, too many foreigners. The future Nazi leader's views were already taking shape, and they would only harden in the coming tumultuous years.

When Germany went to war in August 1914, Hitler enthusiastically signed up with a Bavarian regiment. He later wrote in *Mein Kampf* (My Struggle) about his elation over the thought of going into battle: "Overpowered by stormy enthusiasm, I fell down on my knees and thanked Heaven from an overflowing heart for granting me the good fortune of being permitted to live at this time." Hitler spent four years on the Western Front.

After the armistice, he returned to Munich, once again searching for his path in life. An unforeseen opportunity materialized with the crushing of the Räterepublik. Captain Karl Mayr of the Bavarian army was in need of spies to infiltrate political groups and spot anyone who might be plotting more trouble for Bavarian authorities. Lance Corporal Hitler, with nothing to do with his time, heard about the opportunity. Mayr didn't think much of the disheveled Austrian at first. He later remarked that the young Hitler was "like a stray dog looking for a master." But he signed him up anyway for Abteilung I b/P, Mayr's military intelligence unit.

On the night of September 12, 1919, an obscure cadre of anti-Semites, anti-communists and fervent believers in Germans' ethnic superiority—the German Workers' Party, they called themselves at the time—held a meeting in a back room of a Munich brewery. A stranger in a suit walked in and introduced himself: Adolf Hitler. He had come as part of his mission to collect information on political groups for Captain Mayr. Hitler was at first bored by the discussions, until a professor argued that Bavaria should abandon Germany and form a union with Austria. Hitler asked for permission to speak and then argued forcefully for Bavaria staying with Germany. The leader of this small gathering, Anton Drexler, whispered to a colleague, "This one has a big mouth! We could use him."

Drexler later invited Hitler to speak at party functions. Hitler's beer hall tirades against Jews and the Treaty of Versailles, which had forced reparations on Germany after World War I, struck a chord first with Bavarians of like mind and then with people throughout Germany.

Soon, Hitler was on the radar of the *Munich Post*. The newspaper had become one of the most vocal and devoted champions of the Weimar Republic democracy since its birth. In August 1920, it published an article calling Hitler the "corrupt leader of the German fascists" and saying he was open to bribery. One year later, the newspaper made a huge splash by publishing the text of a scathing pamphlet, anonymously written, that was disseminated by Hitler's rivals within the Nazi Party. The pamphlet raised questions about the sources of all the money Hitler had suddenly come into and his lavish lifestyle. The *Post*'s headline: "Adolf Hitler—Traitor?"

"Just what does he do for a living?" the pamphlet asked. It alleged he was doing the bidding of "shady men behind the scenes" and was using the Nazi Party "solely as a springboard for impure purposes." In their pamphlet, Hitler's Nazi rivals accused him of acting like a "true Jew" in his efforts to take over leadership of the party.

The pamphlet's words gave *Munich Post* readers a remarkable early warning about what was to come: "Do not let yourself be fooled. Hitler is a demagogue, and the only thing that he's any good at is making speeches. He believes with this he can lead the German people astray, and say things that are totally opposite of the truth."

Hitler may have had oratorical skills, but he had sloppy habits, at least in the early years as Nazi leader. This was an embarrassment to some in the Nazi Party as they reached out to members of Munich's high society in the perpetual search for funding. "If you succeeded in making him stand still long enough to confer on important matters, he would take out of his pocket a piece of greasy sausage and a slice of bread, and bolt them while he talked," Kurt Luedecke, one of the Führer's earliest acolytes, wrote in his 1938 book *I Knew Hitler*.

Luedecke, a beret-wearing bon vivant and womanizer, tried to coach him on paying closer attention to his sartorial choices, to appear "less like a refugee" and more like a political leader.

Also taking note of Hitler's slapdash physical appearance and odd demeanor during those early years was Konrad Heiden, who covered the Nazi Party for the *Frankfurter Zeitung*. In his 1944 book, *Der Fuehrer*, written after he fled to the United States, Heiden wrote that when Hitler arrived at a beer hall to give a speech, he "darted down the aisle of yelling supporters with his coat collar turned high." On the speaker's platform, as the gas lamps cast sharp shadows on the beer hall walls, Hitler "was a lank figure, in his shabby black business suit, hardly recognizable from below."

When speaking privately with Luedecke and other confidants, but even in public appearances, Hitler voiced a crass disdain for the opposite sex. He once remarked that women can "love more deeply than men" but a woman has "nothing to do with the intellect."

Despite his uncouthness and misogyny, Hitler had the ability to charm women —including quite a few who held the highest societal positions in Bavaria. He deployed a boyish charisma in his encounters with women who might be of use to him. Some called themselves "Wolf's motherly friends," using a nickname Hitler adopted during the early years in Munich. When visiting these well-heeled ladies in their salons, Hitler would bow and kiss their hands. He displayed a bumpkin-like naivete that some of the women found quaint.

Hitler's unctuousness paid off handsomely. On April 3, 1923, the *Munich Post* reported on the "Hitler-smitten women" who had given or loaned to Hitler not just money, but also "valuable artworks and jewelry."

Among them was Helene Bechstein, wife of piano maker Carl Bechstein. In 1924, she told Munich police investigators who were keeping an eye on Hitler and his benefactors that she had given him "considerable donations." But not money, she said. "I gave him art objects, and noted that he could do with them what he pleased. These were art objects of considerable value."

Hitler typically used such largess as collateral for loans that helped keep the Nazi Party afloat during lean times in the 1920s. A stunning example is documented by a 1923 loan agreement between the Nazis' business manager and German coffee mogul Richard Frank. In return for 600,000 Swiss francs, according to the agreement, "Herr Adolf Hitler transfers to Herr Richard Frank" an "emerald pendant in platinum and brilliants . . . a sapphire ring in platinum and brilliants . . . 14 carat gold ring . . . a red-silk grand piano cover with gold needlework."

Still, Hitler was highly secretive about the sources of the party's funding, and the *Munich Post* persistently used this as a sledgehammer in its reporting on him.

On Monday, March 5, 1923, the presses at Altheimer Eck 19 cranked out copies of the *Post* that contained an anti-Hitler salvo — covering two full pages — that was prompted by a Nazi Party congress recently staged in Munich. The tone was simultaneously mocking and dead serious — classic *Munich Post*.

The article lampooned the Nazis for exaggerating the number of people attending the congress. But it went deeper than that, eviscerating Hitler's posturing as a defender of the working class, essentially accusing him — not Jews — of being the true enemy of the people, and skewering him for the money he was receiving from wealthy Germans.

"The financial means at Herr Hitler's disposal are unusually large," the *Post* article read. The newspaper had obtained a "confidential memo" from a Nazi source stating that in order to increase "Hitler's status within nationalist circles, if he demanded 5 million [marks], he would get it, and immediately."

The *Post* asked: "Why hasn't Hitler answered the repeatedly asked questions about his money sources?"

Gallery One

The Rise of the Nazi Regime

Adolf Hitler leaves a church in Bremerhaven, Germany, circa 1932. (AP Photo)

On the occasion of the last free elections for Reich President, Adolf Hitler gives a speech at a rally of the National Socialists in Lustgarten next to the Berliner Palace, April 4, 1932. (Berliner Verlag/Archiv/picture-alliance/AP Images)

Reich Chancellor Adolf Hitler gives a speech at Garrison Church in Potsdam, Germany, to celebrate the opening of the Reichstag in front of Reich President Paul von Hindenburg, March 21, 1933. (Berliner Verlag/Archiv/picture-alliance/ AP Images)

German chancellor Adolf Hitler speaking to 30,000 uniformed Nazi storm troopers at Kiel, Germany, May 7, 1933. (AP Photo)

Hitler youth honor an unknown soldier by forming a swastika symbol in Germany, August 27, 1933. (AP Photo)

One of the innumerable railway cars arriving at the main station of Nuremberg, Bavaria, for the Reichs-Party Day on September 11, 1933. (AP Photo)

Tens of thousands of Nazi storm troopers take the oath of allegiance to Chancellor Adolf Hitler, in the Lustgarten, Berlin, February 26, 1934. (AP Photo)

Adolf Hitler inspects a line-up of members of the SA during Nuremberg Rally in 1933. (Berliner Verlag/Archiv/ picture-alliance/AP Images)

Swastika banners being carried by storm troopers in white shirts at a pro-Hitler meeting in Saarbrucken, Germany, December 15, 1934. (AP Photo)

While thousands of storm troopers raise hands in salute, Chancellor Adolf Hitler leads his staff down the aisle during opening of the Nazi Party convention in Nuremberg, September 11, 1935. (AP Photo)

Adolf Hitler speaks on the steps of the Altes Museum, Berlin recounting three years of National Socialism in the Reich, January 30, 1936. (AP Photo)

Storm troopers listening to Adolf Hitler on "Brown Shirt Day" at a Nazi Party convention, September 1936. (AP Photo)

The Braunes Haus, (Brown House), headquarters of the Nazi Party in Munich, September 29, 1938. (AP Photo)

Adolf Hitler and his followers visit the Czech defense posts near Neuberbersdorf in Sudetenland in October 1938 after the Munich Agreement of September 29, 1938. (Berliner Verlag/Archiv/picture-alliance/AP Images)

Steel helmets, worn by Adolf Hitler's storm trooper body guard, were lined up on the pavement before the Kroll Opera in Berlin, as the German Reichstag met inside and listened to Hitler's address answering President Roosevelt, April 28, 1939. (AP Photo)

Adolf Hitler speaks at a Munich beer hall that was the scene of the abortive beer hall putsch of 1923, November 8, 1939. (AP Photo)

CHAPTER SEVEN

Hitler Exacts Revenge

"The German revolution has begun," Hitler bellowed, climbing onto a chair in the Bürgerbräukeller. "This hall is surrounded!" The trench-coated Nazi leader and his henchmen had burst in while the leader of the Bavarian government, Gustav Ritter von Kahr, was addressing an audience of finely dressed diners on the evening of November 8, 1923.

Armed men belonging to the Nazis' private militia—the Sturmabteilung, or SA—roared up to the beer hall in trucks. The storm troopers blocked the building exits and mounted a heavy machine gun in the doorway. Kahr and two other officials in the Bavarian government were forced into a back room and told they had to support Hitler in his putsch or face the consequences.

While this political drama played out, another contingent of SA men set off in trucks. Their target: the offices of the *Munich Post*.

Ferdinand Mürriger, the *Post*'s business manager, lived in a third-story apartment at the newspaper's office building. He rushed downstairs at the sound of glass being smashed. It was 11:30 at night.

A mob of about 200 SA men wearing steel helmets and armed with pistols, rifles, and hand grenades had surrounded the building. Aiming a pistol at Mürriger's face, their leader ordered him to open the iron gate. He had no other choice.

A maelstrom of Nazi destruction swept through all three floors of the *Munich Post*. The storm troopers forced open cabinets and drawers. They yanked out ledgers, receipt books, and employees' tax documents. They hurled ink pots against the wall, used their gun butts to smash windows, pulverized desks into unrecognizable piles of wood, and tossed drawers of lead type onto the floor. Just as the violence-drunk SA men were getting ready to go after the printing presses, Bavarian police arrived.

The storm troopers left, but they were not sated. Soon after midnight, more than a dozen of them forced their way into the house of Erhard Auer, the *Post*'s executive editor, their weapons drawn.

A storm trooper wearing a helmet and swastika armband pointed his pistol at the head of Auer's wife. It was about 12:30 in the morning. Also in the house were the Auers' two daughters and their grandson. The Nazi thug demanded to know where Auer was.

"I refuse to tell you," the woman with snow-white hair barked at the SA leader.

Storm troopers burst into the bedroom where the Auers' grandson was asleep. The toddler cried as the SA men used their rifle butts to smash furniture. They wreaked destruction throughout the house.

The family kept their silence about Auer's whereabouts.

"I promise you we will find him," one of the commanders shouted as the storm troopers left.

A truckload of SA troops repeatedly drove up and down the street in front of the Auers' home. On one pass, one of the troopers yelled out, "We'll string you up by your hair."

Hitler's putsch crumbled the next day. With Kahr and the two other Bavarian officials refusing to throw their lot in with the Nazi leader, Hitler decided to march into the heart of the city, hoping to attract crowds of supporters along the way. But when the column of 2,000 putschists reached the Feldherrnhalle, a monument to Bavaria's greatest generals, armed Bavarian state police stood in their way. A shot was fired. And then another. More followed. Putschists at the front of the column fell to the ground. Others fled.

Hitler threw himself to the pavement to duck the flurry of bullets. When it was over, about a dozen of his followers were dead. He himself was whisked away in the car of an SA doctor. Two days later, south of Munich at the home of Ernst Hanfstaengl, a wealthy art patron and a member of Hitler's inner circle, Bavarian state police arrested the Nazi leader.

The SA's raid on the *Munich Post* — and its terrorizing of the Auer family — had a profound impact on the newspaper. In the years ahead, the paper would run articles recounting in detail what had happened that night, trying to stem a resurgence in Hitler's popularity by reminding Germans of the Nazis' wanton destructiveness.

As it turned out, Hitler's arrest and prosecution for high treason would only interrupt his rise, only postpone his return to public life and to history.

It was five days before Christmas 1924 when, granted early parole, Hitler walked out of Landsberg Prison with nearly four years remaining on his five-year sentence. Arriving at his Munich apartment, he was welcomed by friends and followers who had filled the room with food and flowers.

While Hitler had his freedom, the radical right movement was in tatters, riven by fierce disagreements over whether he should lead them. It wasn't just internecine warfare that was sucking energy out of the Nazis; it was also economic and social changes occurring across Germany.

The victors of World War I had agreed to a plan to lessen the crushing financial burden that war reparations payments placed on Germany. The years of hyperinflation were over. A sense of liberation, even of progress, was in the air. New buildings were going up. Customers crowded into department stores. Cafes were busy, and dance halls were packed. Germans were having fun. It looked, for a time, as if Germany's fragile democracy had dodged a bullet. There was less worry about Hitler.

But the *Munich Post* was not ready to sound the all clear. The newspaper printed articles warning that the venom-spewing Nazi leader remained a threat and that he would wait for the right moment to launch another putsch. The paper turned its tormenting of Hitler into something of an art form. Hitler and the Nazis often punched back by filing lawsuits.

When Hitler and his acolytes marched into a Munich court on May 6, 1929, to give testimony in a libel suit against the *Munich Post* and two other news organizations, the *Post* couldn't resist making fun of the spectacle that ensued. The paper took note of the Nazi-sympathizing women who had come to worship their idol, observing that to "call them comely would be going too far." Then the article ridiculed Hitler's appearance in the courtroom. "He was greeted by comically sloppy copies of the fascist greeting," it said, referring to the stiff-arm *Heil Hitler* salute.

Julius Zerfass was the face of the *Munich Post* in court in that case, as the editor responsible for publication of the story. The trial served to highlight suspicions that Hitler was receiving money from Italy in exchange for not laying claim to that country's South Tyrol region, where ethnic Germans formed the majority.

The Nazi leader was among those testifying at the trial. He'd brood or occasionally jump up from his chair and yell at Zerfass and defense lawyer Max Hirschberg. With a pencil and white pads of paper, he drew elaborate sketches of men and women, of knights' helmets, medieval armor and more, including "Norman boats with sails swelled out widely and fluttering banners," the judge in the case, Hans Frank, wrote in his memoirs.

Hitler angrily defended his relationship with Mussolini, the Italian dictator, but called the allegation that he was receiving Italian payments a "dirty slur."

The *Post* lost the lawsuit. The fine the newspaper was ordered to pay was small. But for Zerfass, a far greater penalty for his anti-Hitler agitation at the *Post* lay ahead. The Nazis would send him to Dachau, and his life would never be the same.

CHAPTER EIGHT

Stab In The Back

Statute books were piled up on a table in the courtroom, and Max Hirschberg, the finely dressed defense lawyer who'd represented the *Munich Post* many times, perused memos and other papers one more time, making occasional notations. Seated at his side, Martin Gruber, his stocky, pince-nez-wearing editor-client, surveyed the scene and waited, trying not to fidget. One of the most publicized trials in Germany in the 20th century was about to get underway. It would be known as the Stab In The Back trial.

There were many in Germany who were in denial about the causes of their country's defeat in World War I almost seven years earlier and who endorsed a claim floating around among nationalists, generals, and the extreme-right. Their claim was that Germany had been "stabbed in the back" by the Social Democrats in 1918 by accepting the harsh terms of an armistice instead of letting military leaders launch new offensives against the Allies and negotiate a better deal.

Hitler was among those who had been repeating the lie. Gesticulating wildly at his rallies, the Führer would fulminate about what he called the "November Criminals"—the leftist politicians who supposedly sold out their country.

The so-called Stab In The Back (*Dolchstoss* in German) thesis was vigorously promoted in two successive editions of a Munich-based magazine, the *Süddeutsche Monatshefte* (*South German Monthly Magazine*), in the spring of 1924. On the cover of the April edition was an illustration showing a German soldier lying on the ground with a dagger in his neck.

The *Munich Post* responded with a series of articles that accused the magazine editor, Paul Cossmann, of intentionally falsifying history. Cossmann sued the *Post* for libel.

The *Dolchstoss* trial began on October 19, 1925. Reporters from across the country and even from abroad were in the courtroom to cover the historic legal contest. The world paid attention as the two sides argued over who was to blame for Germany's defeat and the political, social and economic upheavals that followed.

Hirschberg called historians, leading Social Democrats, and the last commander of German military forces during the closing days of the war, General Wilhelm Groener, to speak in defense of the *Munich Post's* assertion that Cossmann had falsified history. The defense lawyer's marshalling of facts, figures and testimony from unimpeachable sources overwhelmingly made the case that it was the German military that wanted the war stopped because of its enormous losses on the battlefield.

"The Stab In The Back problem is today absolutely resolved historically," Hirschberg said, according to a biography of him, *Justice Imperiled*, by American attorney Douglas G. Morris.

Among the witnesses testifying for Cossmann were military officers who were associates of the magazine editor and felt their reputations were harmed. When questioned by Hirschberg, according to Morris' book, many gave evasive answers or said they couldn't remember.

"I have another view. I simply cannot verify it with evidence," a lieutenant general replied when asked by Hirschberg to explain his belief in the *Dolchstoss* when military experts had testified that the war was lost on the battlefield.

Cossmann had claimed that his honor was attacked by the *Munich Post* articles. Hirschberg turned that around, arguing that it was Cossmann who was showing dishonor by failing to recognize the sacrifices of normal soldiers who had served on the front lines. The valor of those soldiers in the face of impending defeat was, he said, "a page of honor for the German people and the German army that should not be besmirched or defiled by the Stab in the Back contention," according to Morris' book.

One witness testifying for the *Post*'s defense was Ludwig Rudolph, a schoolteacher who had fought in World War I. Rudolph, according to Morris, told the court he had volunteered to testify because he was beside himself that in this trial those who had directly experienced the war seemed "damned to silence."

Cossmann was left arguing that scholarship would never be able to say whether Germany could have avoided defeat. But he said he believed that "the war would have been won if the whole German nation had stood together and directed its whole will toward the victorious ending of the war," Morris' book says.

On Dec. 9, 1925, Judge Albert Frank ruled that the articles published by Cossmann did indeed contain numerous errors. But Frank also ruled that evidence presented at the trial failed to prove that Cossmann had intentionally falsified history. Frank found Gruber guilty of defaming Cossmann and ordered the

Munich Post managing editor to pay 3,000 Reichmarks.

Hirschberg and Cossmann personified some of the divisions that plagued the Weimar Republic's fragile democracy.

Hirschberg was born into a prominent Jewish family that had assimilated into German culture. His mother came from a banking family and his father was founder of a major Munich fashion house. Hirschberg studied law in Berlin and Leipzig before finishing his law degree with high honors in Munich in 1910.

Hirschberg had a law practice in Munich when he was mobilized on August 24, 1914. It's hard to imagine now, but young men on both sides in World War I — the Allies and the Central Powers — eagerly signed up for military service, motivated by zealous patriotism and a romanticized view of going into battle. Hirschberg was among the masses of young men stirred to go off and fight for their homelands.

He rose through the ranks while fighting on the Western Front, eventually becoming commander of an antiaircraft battalion. He was decorated for valor — for riding to aid fellow soldiers who had been left behind as bombs exploded around him and for shooting down more airplanes than other antiaircraft battery commanders. He read Dostoyevsky, Kierkegaard and Schopenhauer while in the trenches, and comrades admired the death-defying attitude he demonstrated.

Because of his war experiences, Hirschberg developed pacifist views and devoted himself to socialist causes. Returning to his law practice in Munich, he defended leftist workers who had been arrested by Bavaria's reactionary government for their involvement in the ill-starred Räterepublik and he received death threats for being their champion.

Three years before the *Dolchstoss* libel trial, Hirschberg

defended a leading socialist, Felix Fechenbach, against a charge of treason. Fechenbach had been Kurt Eisner's secretary before Eisner's murder. He was charged by Bavarian officials in 1922 with leaking sensitive German documents to a French journalist, who published them. Hirschberg lost the case — Fechenbach was sentenced to 11 years in prison — but devoted himself to fighting what was clearly an unjust verdict. The Bavarian government pardoned Fechenbach in December 1924 but put him on probation for the remainder of his jail term and refused to erase the mark on his record. Adolf Hitler was freed from Landsberg prison on the same day.

Like Hirschberg, Cossmann was born to a prominent Jewish family. His father, Bernhard Cossmann, was an accomplished cellist and close friend of the great Russian composer Pyotr Tchaikovsky, whom he knew from his time teaching at the Moscow Conservatory. On Tchaikovsky's visits to Germany, he would visit the Cossmanns.

Paul Cossmann converted from Judaism to Roman Catholicism in 1905. One year earlier, he founded the *Süddeutsche Monatshefte*. Until the start of World War I, the magazine was a respected showcase of quality writing on literary and cultural matters. Thomas Mann was among the early contributors.

Although Cossmann did not fight in the war, his magazine became a cheerleader for German militarism. Cossmann was no defender of violence perpetrated by the radical right. But his magazine did provide the extremists with an intellectual foundation with its articles rejecting the idea that Germany bore guilt for starting the war and blaming leftists for the Germans' defeat.

By the time the Stab In The Back trial occurred, Bavaria had become a toxic hatchery of anti-Semitic, radical-right groups like the German Workers' Party, a place where attacks on socialists could go unpunished, where right-wing extremists could get away with hoarding guns in secret caches, and where those who espoused anti-left principles could find sympathy with judges. After he got out of prison for the abortive Beer Hall Putsch, Hitler put the Stab In The Back lie to effective use during his climb to power. While Germans were debating whether they were defeated because of a *Dolchstoss*, it was German democracy that was getting stabbed in the back.

The famous trial was not to be the last time Hirschberg and *Munich Post* editors would team up to fight libel accusations over articles that targeted ultranationalist and extremist views. Hirschberg spent so much time on *Munich Post* cases that he was almost like a member of the staff. While the editors attacked Hitler with the typewritten word, Max Hirschberg went after the Nazis with the law.

CHAPTER NINE

Return of the Brown Menace

A large sack bobbed in the icy waters of a reservoir near Dresden on the day after Christmas, 1932. Passersby spotted the bulky object and alerted police, noticing that its contents had a human shape. Wrapped inside the cocoon of death was the body of Herbert Hentsch. The 26-year-old's hands and feet had been tied. A bullet wound was in his chest.

Hentsch, a member of the brown-shirted Sturmabteilung, had disappeared nearly two months earlier. The grisly discovery of his body brought suspicion onto his Nazi colleagues.

An investigation showed that three SA comrades lured Hentsch to the location, killed him and threw his body into the reservoir. Hentsch had somehow run afoul of his fellow Nazis. The suspected murderers fled to Italy.

The *Munich Post* saw an opportunity to turn up the heat on Hitler. The Nazi Führer had been silent on Hentsch's killing. The *Munich Post* wanted to know why. It said it was Hitler's obligation to get the trio to return to Germany.

"What have you done toward solving this murder, Herr Hitler? This question will be repeatedly raised. But one can already see that Hitler and the NSDAP have done nothing to explain the killing," the *Post* wrote in an article published on January 21, 1933.

Earlier that month, the *Post*'s coverage of the murder took up nearly the whole front page. The January 21 article reprinted an astonishing obituary written by Hentsch's mother and first published in Dresden newspapers. In the obituary, the grieving woman pleaded with German mothers to keep their sons from becoming Nazis.

"I deeply regret that I did not warn my dear child against running with this crowd," the mother wrote. "I call on all mothers to protect their children from these elements."

The death of Herbert Hentsch was just one murder in a daily spree of political violence that killed hundreds during the final years of the Weimar Republic. Nazis and communists attacked each other on the street and at rallies. Nazi storm troopers also targeted members of the Social Democratic Party. They even attacked each other.

The Great Depression threw millions of Germans out of work and sowed political chaos. Because of anger over the central government's inability to deal with the economic crisis, the extremist Nazi and Communist parties appealed to a growing number of voters. Especially alarming was Hitler's surge in popularity. The Nazis had won just 2.6 percent of the vote in parliamentary elections in May 1928 but 37.4 percent in July 1932 elections, becoming the largest party in the Reichstag. When he ran for president in 1932, Hitler lost to incumbent Paul von Hindenburg, but the Nazi leader still won the approval of more than 13 million Germans—37 percent of the ballots cast.

While other newspapers showed growing concern about Hitler, the *Munich Post* repeatedly attacked him on its front pages. Hitler had long claimed the Nazis were not involved in any illegal activities. But to the *Munich Post*, the Nazi Party was above all else a criminal organization, from bottom to top. And the paper set about proving it with the zeal of a prosecutor.

Daily rundowns on the latest political killings and other acts of violence around the nation filled the *Post*'s pages, often with provocative headlines:

"Hitler's Murder Bandits"

"A Monstrous Nazi Crime"

"The Criminal Activities of the Hitler Party"

"Political Murders: Eight New Victims"

Periodically, the *Post* would tally up the murders and publish the names of the victims, and where and when they died. One such list, headlined "Two Years Of Nazi Murders," took up all of Page 3 in the December 8, 1931, editions. A thick black border gives a funereal look to the list, which does not provide the circumstances of the deaths, other than to say "murdered by Nazis." Clearly, the list implies, within the Nazi Party beat many a murderous heart. At the bottom of the full-page chronology of deaths is this, printed in big, bold letters: "Stop the Nazi Murder Pestilence!"

From the early years of the Nazi Party, the *Munich Post* published lists like this. Just two days after storm troopers raided and ransacked the newspaper's offices on the night of November 8, 1923, during Hitler's failed Beer Hall Putsch, the *Munich Post* published a long chronology of acts of violence in Bavaria that had been perpetrated by Nazis and their extreme-right predecessors since 1920. By running the chronology of about 90 violent acts, the *Post* was making the point that too little had been done to crack down on the Nazis.

It would have been rare for a Nazi crime to have escaped the attention of the *Munich Post*.

On July 11, 1932, the newspaper published a story about a man named Berger, one of 25 National Socialists who got into a shootout in the northern city of Hagen with some communists. From his jail cell, the arrested man wrote a letter informing on multiple low-level Nazis for crimes he knew they had committed.

The *Post* caustically commented: "Berger joined the National Socialists because he believed in their idealism and the dignity of their goals. And now he is calling his former comrades burglars, pimps, pickpockets, check kiters, muggers and perjurers."

On October 8, 1932, the newspaper reported on the murder of a 19-year-old named Emma by her 23-year-old Hitler Youth boyfriend and two of his comrades. Emma, a maid living in Frankfurt, was pregnant when she disappeared in December 1931. Her corpse was discovered five months later in the Main River, which flows through Frankfurt.

Police and relatives had assumed that Emma had killed herself by jumping into the river, the *Post* reported. The truth was discovered completely by happenstance.

A sister of Emma found two letters that the deceased woman had written and addressed to a certain "Robert" just before she disappeared. In the letters, Emma wrote that she was pregnant with Robert's child and that she knew he would not marry her. Emma wrote that the least Robert could do was give her some financial support, since the child was his.

One day in September 1932, Emma's two sisters were dining at a Frankfurt café. A young man who walked in got into conversation with them, introducing himself as Robert. "Are you, perhaps, the man to whom my sister wrote letters?" one of them asked him. Robert reacted with "bewildered surprise, severe agitation and obvious lies," the *Post* reported.

The sisters reported their suspicions to Frankfurt police. When they picked up Robert for questioning, he confessed to killing Emma with the help of two friends. The three gave a chilling account of the cold-blooded murder. When Robert approached the two fellow Hitler Youth members about how to deal with Emma, one suggested shooting her, according to the *Post*. The other proposed throwing her off a bridge over the Main. Preferring that plan, Robert asked Emma to go for a night-time stroll along the river, his two accomplices following at a distance on bicycles.

"And here is the most unimaginable and horrific thing about this crime," the *Post* wrote. "He had sex with his victim just before murdering her."

When Robert tried to push her off a bridge over the Main, the article continued, Emma "resisted with all of her might, clinging to her loved one" and to the bridge — before she plunged into the river and disappeared.

In its research, the *Post* learned that in May 1932 Robert was part of a gang of Nazis who brutally attacked a 60-year-old Social Democrat and left him with serious injuries.

The *Munich Post*, which often had the sassy appeal of a tabloid, did not shy away from lurid stories like those about Herbert Hentsch and the unfortunate Emma. Then as now, sex and violence sell. But there is something far deeper happening here. Behind every anti-Nazi article published by the *Post*, there was the hope that Germans who were drawn to Hitler would see that he and his party were the root cause of the collapse of law and order across the nation.

Ever since the *Post* dared in 1906 to call out Carl Peters for his atrocities — and even before then — the leftist newspaper relished going after authoritarian types. Looking back on the history of the spunky publication, this is remarkable: When the *Post's* opponents fought back, to the point that the editors' lives were endangered, the newspaper would often come back with more dirt, with more scandalous revelations, with more warnings about dangers that lay ahead for their homeland.

CHAPTER TEN

"The Solution of the Jewish Question"

For years, the *Munich Post* editors printed whatever they could to raise the anti-Nazi alarm, but their edition of December 9, 1931, still provides a searing shock for its reportage and the headline on one particular story. For Munich readers that day and for others generations later, it presents a black-and-white refutation of claims that would be made by Germans after the Second World War that they didn't know about Hitler's nefarious plans for Jews.

"The (Nazi) party leadership . . . has, for the eventuality of taking power, drafted special guidelines for the 'Solution of The Jewish Question,'" the *Post* reported, noting that the plans were being kept secret by the Nazi leaders.

"For tactical reasons, all public discussion of the Jewish question has been put off. They fear a foreign policy impact, in London and Paris, but practically speaking, there is an exact plan" for all of Germany, the newspaper said.

The article, running under a startling boldface headline that no reader could miss —"Jews in the Third Reich"—then proceeded to quote from that secret plan:

"All Jews living in Germany have no right to citizenship . . . No Jew can have a civil service job . . . A Jew cannot give testimony in a German court . . . All Jews living in Germany will be placed under special laws. They are to pay a special tax . . . Medical treatment of Christians by Jews is not allowed. Marriages between Jews and Christians will be declared invalid. Jewish children are not allowed to attend German schools or universities."

And there was more.

Germany would reserve the right to "intern or deport" undesirable "Jewish denizens" who violate the "interests of the German Volk."

As a "final solution" of how to deal with German Jews, the newspaper reported, "it is proposed to use Jews in Germany for labor and reclaiming German moorlands . . . with the SS watching over them."

It is chilling how close what actually happened during the Holocaust comes to the Nazi guidelines disclosed by the *Munich Post*. There is no mention in the guidelines of setting up death camps — like Auschwitz — in countries to be occupied by the Nazis, or of massacring Jewish men, women and children in East European towns and burying them in mass graves. The specifics of those actions were worked out by the Nazi leadership after Germany invaded its neighbors to the east.

Nonetheless, the "guidelines" published by the *Post* offer a foretaste of the Nuremberg Race Laws of 1935 that stripped Jews of their basic rights and set the stage for the Holocaust.

"Jews In The Third Reich" was among a cluster of articles published by the *Post* over a period of a few months about Nazi thinking on how to deal with the "Jewish Question." Others dealt with the problem of how do you identify a Jew?

In an article published January 12, 1932, under the blunt headline "Eugenics In The Third Reich," the *Post* reported on a Leipzig conference of a Nazi doctors' association. The *Post* got its information by reading reports on the conference published in Nazi newspapers. To get readers' attention, the *Post's* article started with this:

"Humans can be classified according to their size, weight, athletic ability, the color of their eyes or their hair. But can humans be classified by the percentage of Jewish blood? In Herr Hitler's Third Reich, it is seriously intended that German citizenship can be denied based on the amount of Jewish blood coursing through someone's veins."

The featured speaker at the Nazi physicians' conference was a Dr. Staemmler, who opened his lecture by discussing the dangers of allowing "inferior" Jews and Germans to breed. It was bad enough that over the decades such coupling had already occurred, but it had to be stopped, in the opinion of Dr. Staemmler. Marriages between Germans and Jews must be made illegal.

But how to determine who is a Jew?

Dr. Staemmler described to the gathering of fascist, anti-Semitic physicians how that could be accomplished: by determining the amount of Jewish blood in a person's body through lineage. It was simple math.

It is agreed, he argued, that someone with two Jewish parents is also a Jew, even if either or both parents had converted to Christianity. The same goes for a person with one Jewish parent, he said. "There is a view," he said, that "to be German" the most Jewish blood you could have would be from one great-grandparent."

Germans and Jews should face prison sentences if they have nonmarital sex, said Dr. Staemmler. Serial criminals, prostitutes and those suffering from inheritable diseases should be sterilized, whether Jewish or not.

The Nazi doctors' conference ended with a word from Gregor Strasser, a Hitler confidant and a leading Nazi official. "In Professor Staemmler's lecture," he said, "there was not a single sentence that could not be realized, even put into effect very quickly."

Four days before that article appeared, the *Post* published a story showing how some of the ideas presented by Dr. Staemmler were already being put into practice by the Nazi SS, the paramilitary organization commanded by Heinrich Himmler.

The headline on the article published on January 8, 1932, was "Nazi Breeding Facility." The subhead read: "Foretaste Of The Third Reich." The article concerned "SS Order No. 65," dated December 31, 1931, and issued at Nazi headquarters in Munich. The order announced to SS members that henceforth before they married they had to obtain Himmler's consent.

No SS man would be allowed to marry a "racially inferior woman," the order stated, nor could an SS man become engaged without first checking with an SS specialist appointed to handle race matters.

The goal, stated SS Order No. 65, was a "precious people that is free of hereditary disease" and with Nordic and German characteristics. "The future of the Volk depends upon the selection and preservation of . . . good blood."

To ensure the blood of SS families was kept pure, members were required to submit comprehensive genealogical reports on themselves and their prospective brides and documents proving they are free of hereditary disease, among other things. After Himmler gave his blessing to the union, full racial and ancestral details on the couple would be entered into an SS registry.

Any SS man who violated SS Order No. 65 would be kicked out of the paramilitary organization.

The *Munich Post* continued reporting on this theme on May 6, 1932, with an article, headlined "National Socialist Race Mania," comparing Nazis' obsession with creating a pure race to the work of a mad scientist. The piece contained more details on Nazi musings for ways to keep the German race pure, again methods that were used after Hitler's rise to power.

On July 23, 1932, the *Post* published an article saying the Nazis were planning nothing less than a "prison state." The newspaper cited a secret document that discussed, among other things, setting up "collection camps for people who are unwilling to work or are politically unreliable." They would be guarded by SS and SA troops.

Once again, the *Munich Post* foreshadowed the perfidious times to come.

CHAPTER ELEVEN

Vermin in the Brown House

Max Hirschberg stood up in a Munich court and delivered a blistering indictment of Hitler and the Nazi Party. It was April 1, 1932, and once again Martin Gruber was at his side. Hirschberg was defending the *Munich Post* against a libel lawsuit over the newspaper's revelation that the Nazis had put together lists of people to be assassinated if Hitler came to power. The *Post* had printed the hit list on the front page.

A cannonade of damning facts bolstered Hirschberg's argument. He named murderers who were members of the Nazi Party and presented a long list of Nazis who had used firearms to commit violent crimes. He made use of articles in the Nazis' newspapers and quotes from party officials, including Hitler himself.

Hirschberg read from a "songbook" handed out to members of the paramilitary Sturmabteilung. On page 9, Hirschberg told the court, was this line from an SA "battle song":

"For the race war, columns of storm troopers are standing at the ready,

Only when the Jews bleed will we be free."

From a Nazi newspaper in Berlin, Hirschberg quoted: "Catastrophe is coming, because it must come." The paper went on: "We will make sure that it's not the immortal German Volk who are buried beneath the rubble, but those good-for-nothing politicians" who had been running the country since Germany's World War I defeat.

All the evidence, Hirschberg said, showed that Hitler and his henchmen had "organized and approved politically motivated murders and other acts of violence in preparation for a violent coup."

The trial lasted less than a week. In the end, the court ignored Hirschberg's rigorous documentation that Hitler was bent on overthrowing the Weimar democracy. Siding with claims by Nazi functionaries who testified that the hit list was a fake, the court fined Gruber 2,000 Reichsmarks.

The *Post* was undeterred. Just two days after losing the libel case, the newspaper published yet another blockbuster to rattle the Brown House, the Nazi Party's headquarters. The *Post* had obtained information that a secret Nazi cell had been formed to assassinate SA chief Ernst Röhm and four of his closest associates: Georg Bell, Hans Erwin von Spreti-Weilbach, Julius Uhl, and Karl Leon Du Moulin-Eckart.

The *Post* described a plot in which high-ranking Nazi officials — acting like Mafia dons — planned to use low-level Nazis to carry out the hits. Conspirators used the code names "Helene," "Wieland II" and "Wieland I." A letter describing the plan referred to an assassin dubbed "fat bunny" who would be "dressed warmly," parlance for having a gun. For another intended victim, the conspirators had in mind a car accident. The spindle would be loosened on a wheel of his Opel, the wheel would fly off, and the vehicle would careen out of control.

The attacks were never carried out, although the *Post* could not claim credit for thwarting the plot. Struck by a pang of conscience, one of the conspirators showed the letter outlining the assassination plans to one of the intended victims. The would be-victim went to the police. It is also possible that police got earlier word from an informer inside the Brown House. In any event, police arrested four suspects on April 7 and 8.

The *Post's* pursuit of this bizarre plot, as with numerous others, was not just to show the criminality of the Nazis, but to drive wedges into the Brown House by revealing mortal rivalries among Hitler's followers.

There is a larger story surrounding the plot to kill Röhm and his closest confidants, one laced with blackmail, conspiracies, perfidy, and Machiavellian jockeying for power among Hitler's minions. And the *Munich Post* was on top of it the whole time it was playing out.

It started on June 22, 1931, when the *Munich Post* ran this front-page banner headline: "Warm Brotherhood in the Brown House," with the subhead, "Sex Lives in the Third Reich."

The Brown House was rocked by the story that followed. While the Nazi Party had been pushing for a crackdown on homosexuality, the *Post* reported, one of their own — Röhm — had been caught in a blackmailing scheme that resulted in the revelation that he himself was homosexual.

The *Post* had obtained a letter from a Nazi intelligence officer, a Dr. Meyer, to Röhm in which Meyer recounted meetings he had held with the SA chief. The putative purpose of the letter was to confirm what Meyer had heard in the meetings. The real intent was blackmail.

Meyer reminded Röhm that the SA leader had told him of his two years as a military advisor in Bolivia and that the SA chief had boasted that although "homosexuality was something unknown there ...you had been working to make fast and lasting changes in this area." Meyer also reminded Röhm that the SA boss asked if he could help him out of a potentially embarrassing predicament involving a Dr. Heimsoth.

The *Post* report went on, quoting the letter in unsparing detail. "You mentioned that you had inadvertently gone with Dr. Heimsoth to homosexual bars to meet homosexual boys and pick them up," Meyer wrote in the blackmail letter. He also noted that Röhm had confided that he and Dr. Heimsoth liked to look at "artistically valuable collections of homoerotic photos." Dr. Heimsoth had in his possession compromising letters written by Röhm that he would like to get back, the SA chief told Meyer.

Meyer paid a visit to Dr. Heimsoth who, after a brief chat, mentioned that he had sent a letter to Röhm asking him for funds to start up a news service and he had not received a response. Meyer told Dr. Heimsoth that Röhm had been preoccupied with an internal revolt within the SA.

When Meyer and Röhm met the next day, the SA chief was unhappy that Meyer did not have the compromising letters. "They must be obtained at all costs," he told Meyer, who promised to try again to get the letters back.

This is where Karl Mayr—the ex-Bavarian army captain who hired Hitler as an intelligence officer way back before the Nazi Party was formed—comes in. And this is where the story loops back to the *Post*'s reporting on the murder squad, "Cell G," that was supposedly created to assassinate Röhm and his circle.

Two top Nazis named by the *Post* in its stories on "Cell G"—Paul Schulz and Franz Xaver Schwarz—sued the newspaper for suggesting that they were the main conspirators to kill Röhm and his associates. The trial began on Monday, October 3, 1932. Hirschberg was once again defending the *Post* and its political editor, Edmund Goldschagg.

At this libel trial, dark secrets about back-stabbing, conspiracies and envy within the Brown House entered the glaring light of day. The trial showed there was indeed a Nazi plot to kill Röhm's closest aides—and quite possibly Röhm himself—to weaken the power of the storm troopers.

Karl Mayr appears to have been a major source for the *Post's* reporting on "Cell G." Mayr was an early member of the Nazi Party but ended up joining the Social Democratic Party in 1925. He became a leader of the Social Democrats' self-defense force, the *Reichsbanner Schwarz-Rot-Gold*, and the editor of the organization's newspaper.

Mayr testified that in late 1931 he had received an "article" offered by a man who said he was involved in the training of a "Cell G" operated by the National Socialists. The sender said a multi-day conference of "Cell G's" functionaries had met at the Brown House and that Hitler welcomed them personally. Mayr told the court he was suspicious of being fed misinformation—possibly by communists—and so he didn't publish it in the Reichsbanner's newspaper. The *Post* got the same information and ran with it.

Mayr told the court he decided to check with Georg Bell, one of the Röhm aides allegedly targeted for assassination, who confirmed the substance of the information sent to Mayr about "Cell

G." Mayr was still skeptical. Bell said Röhm had more information and he'd set up a meeting with him.

When Röhm and Mayr met for about three hours at a Berlin hotel, the SA leader confirmed that what Mayr had been told about "Cell G" was "by and large true." He then ranted about several Nazi functionaries he was certain were behind the plot, as well as "other dirty tricks" occurring within the Brown House, according to Mayr's testimony.

In his own testimony, Bell said Röhm had told him of a plot to kill the two of them plus Du Moulin-Eckart. "I couldn't believe this, until Röhm told me details," Bell said.

Röhm told him that Schwarz and Schulz—the two plaintiffs in the libel case against the *Post*—were masterminds of the plot, Bell testified.

As the *Post's* lawyer, Hirschberg was vexed by the failure of many important witnesses to comply with requests that they come to court to testify. Hitler transferred Du Moulin-Eckart to the Nazi offices in Vienna. Through his attorney, Röhm told the Munich court he wouldn't be able to testify because he was also in Vienna. Nazis allegedly involved in the conspiracy also failed to appear.

The trial lasted just one day. Schwarz and Schulz won the case. The judge ruled that there was insufficient evidence that they were conspirators in the murder scheme, as claimed by the *Munich Post*. The *Post* was fined 1,200 Reichsmarks.

The *Post* did appear to go too far with playing up the alleged roles of Schwarz and Schulz. Historians believe that another high-ranking Nazi, Walter Buch, was the kingpin in the murder plot, and if Schwarz and Schulz were involved they probably had minor roles. Only one person was held to account for the murder plan: Emil Danzeisen, one of the four arrested in early April of 1932, was sentenced to just six months in jail.

The verdict reflected the way the Bavarian judicial system worked in those troubled times. It was shown time and time again in libel cases against the *Munich Post*—at the Stab In The Back trial of 1925, the 1929 trial that examined whether Hitler was getting money from Mussolini, the April 1932 trial over publication of a hit list, and six months later, the loss to Schwarz and Schulz.

Just as the swastika-bedecked neoclassical stone mansion known as the Brown House was infested with murderers and plotters, likewise the Bavarian justice system was infested with right-wing judges all too willing to let Hitler and his lackeys off the hook.

Nonetheless, even in its courtroom defeats, the *Munich Post* was a winner. Even though the *Post* was playing defense, the trial strategies of Max Hirschberg served to shine a searchlight into the dark corners of the malevolent Brown House.

CHAPTER TWELVE

Democracy Dismembered

Looking like menacing specters in the night, more than 20,000 storm troopers, SS men and World War I veterans marched in a torchlight parade through Berlin on January 30, 1933, jubilant over Adolf Hitler's appointment that day as German chancellor. Red flags with swastikas waved, and "Deutschland Über Alles" filled the air.

The night-time spectacle was choreographed by Nazi propaganda chief Joseph Goebbels, who had perfected the art of bringing Hitler's message directly to the people through mass rallies and radio broadcasts.

Hitler rose to the chancellor position — the German equivalent of prime minister — through a backroom deal with businessmen, military officers and right-wing politicians who thought they would be able to control him and get him to do their bidding. The coalition government was divided among the Nazis, the German National Peoples' Party, a right-wing paramilitary organization called the Steel Helmets, and conservatives with no party affiliation. The coalition had a vice chancellor: Fritz von Papen, a former chancellor and ultranationalist who persuaded

President Paul von Hindenburg to appoint Hitler chancellor.

Hitler's sudden ascension to the top political office in the land left journalists scrambling to try to foresee what would happen next. Two major Berlin-based, liberal dailies that had defended the Weimar Republic, the *Vossische Zeitung* and the *Berliner Tageblatt*, said Germans should brace for the worst.

Theodor Wolff, a columnist for the *Tageblatt*, wrote that there were "people sitting in the Cabinet who for weeks and months" had spoken out for "breaking with the constitution, doing away with the Reichstag, muzzling the opposition, and an unfettered use of dictatorial force."

The *Vossische Zeitung* warned: "One cannot end poverty, but one can end freedom. Misery cannot be banned, but the press can be. Hunger will not be banished, but Jews can be."

Socialist newspapers, the *Munich Post* included, exhorted workers to turn out en masse for parliamentary elections called by Hitler for March 5. "If fascism wins, basic citizens' rights will come to an end for the foreseeable future," the *Post* wrote.

Newspapers popular with the middle class were willing, and a number of them eager, to give Hitler a chance to show whether he had the skills to end Germany's soaring unemployment and address other woes besetting the nation.

"Stay Calm!" the *Berliner Morgenpost* newspaper said in its lead story the day after Hitler became chancellor. The newspaper *Germania*, voice of the Catholic-dominated Center Party, said: "Herr Hitler must now show what he's capable of achieving." Many papers opined that they were certain that the Nazis' coalition partners would be able to "tame" Hitler — to rein him in and keep him from pushing through extremist policies.

It took Hitler little time to show that he had been seriously underestimated. Unleashed by the Führer's elevation to the chancellor's office, the Nazis' paramilitary units acted with abandon. Left-wingers, trade union offices, Communists and Social Democrats were assaulted by storm troopers who no longer had any reason to fear the possibility of charges. The Social Democratic mayor of Stassfurt was killed by a Nazi on February 5. Being a Social Democrat—as were the editors of the *Munich Post*—meant not knowing whether you might be next.

Der Führer quickly started putting together the building blocks of a propaganda structure that would use government resources to sway Germans' emotions and intimidate the non-Nazi news media. Goebbels was named head of the newly created Reich Ministry for The People's Education and Propaganda, putting him in a position to bring newspapers into line with the Nazi way of thinking.

Hitler's first official assault on press freedoms came on February 4, 1933, just days after his elevation, with the government coalition's approval of a decree cynically titled "For the Protection of the German People." The ordinance gave Interior Minister Wilhelm Frick, a veteran Nazi, power to suspend the publication of newspapers that were seen as a threat, at least in Hitler's view. Across the country, the Nazis went after newspapers that dared to oppose Hitler, banning some for a week or two or completely shutting them down.

"This Is How the Press Is Muzzled," read a headline in the *Munich Post*.

Then an incident on February 27 catalyzed this dark trend: A Dutch anarchist torched the Reichstag, Germany's national parliament. Playing on Germans' fears, Hitler claimed the conflagration was the start of a Communist plot to take over the country. With Germany reeling from soaring unemployment and economic instability, the desire for a strongman as leader was only deepened by the Reichstag fire. And Hitler readily exploited the conflagration to tighten his grip. About 4,000 Communists were arrested. And on February 28, Hitler's cabinet approved an emergency decree —known as the Reichstag Fire Decree —that suspended many of the civil liberties that were pillars of Germany's democratic constitution. Among them: guarantees of a free press and freedom of assembly.

Even before the Reichstag fire, Frick let Bavarian authorities know that he would begin suspending unfriendly newspapers there. On February 26, Munich police said the *Munich Post* would be suspended for four days under the Feb. 4 decree "For the "Protection of the German People." Frick had demanded a suspension of eight days. Bavarian authorities tried to exercise some of their state powers by agreeing to four.

The presses at Altheimer Eck 19 went silent on February 27, the day of the Reichstag fire. They started back up again with a vengeance.

"We Will Not Be Intimidated!" screamed the banner headline on the front page of the March 3 edition. The four-day ban was "totally unjustified," the *Post*'s article said, because the newspaper was just reporting the truth.

"The *Munich Post* will continue to engage in a battle, a battle for Social Democracy and for the freedom-loving working class," the article read.

Parliamentary elections were held on March 5. Nazis won 43.9 percent of the vote, and votes for his coalition partners gave Hitler a parliamentary majority. He still didn't have absolute power. But by now he was unstoppable.

Hitler was murdering German democracy, methodically cutting out its organs. The rights of Germany's states were protected by the constitution that created the Weimar democracy. That had to change for Hitler to have absolute power. Some of the northern states already had Nazi leaders. Others fell in line, with Hitler appointing Nazi friends to replace elected officials who had been governing states. Storm troopers terrorized the populace to scare off anyone who might decide to take a stand against Nazi rule.

Bavaria was the last state to fall. Although the Nazi movement had begun there, Bavarians' historically did not like being told what to do by Berlin. Many would have preferred restoration of the Bavarian monarchy over being ruled by Hitler. The Nazis made a promise to leave Bavaria alone, but they broke it.

CHAPTER THIRTEEN

"Enemies of the State and of the People"

When the overnight train from Berlin pulled into Munich's Hauptbahnhof at 8:20 in the morning, two Nazi officials, SA leader Ernst Röhm and Adolf Wagner, stepped off and soon were met by SS chief Heinrich Himmler. It was March 9, 1933, and they were on a mission for Germany's new chancellor, Adolf Hitler, who was aggressively consolidating his power.

Dressed in their crisp Nazi uniforms, the three left the station for the offices of Bavaria's minister president, Dr. Heinrich Held, to demand his resignation. Held refused —but there would be no stopping the Nazis' plans for control of Bavaria, of Munich and of anyone, including political figures and journalists, who would try to get in their way.

As the day wore on, signs of the new order grew more obvious and ominous. A large crowd of Nazi supporters gathered on Marienplatz, the expansive main square in front of New City Hall, and two local Hitler henchmen, Max Amann and Christian Weber, marched in with a red swastika banner about 20 feet long. They hung it from the building's tower as the growing mass in the square cheered and applauded. Amann appeared on a balcony wearing a swastika armband on his right arm, and he announced to the assembly below that the leadership of the Bavarian government was being taken over by General Ritter von Epp, a Bavarian native and veteran Nazi, and that Himmler was taking over as head of Bavarian police.

All the while, the Sturmabteilung got busy dealing with real and perceived threats to Hitler—chasing, assaulting, and arresting Social Democrats, Communists, Jews, and others, a campaign that would not let up in the coming months.

That evening, as the Nazis' Bavarian coup unfolded, *Munich Post* editor in chief Erhard Auer held a secret meeting with other Social Democrat leaders in the back room of a tavern on Lenbachplatz, just a few blocks from his newspaper's office. A heavy cloth curtain veiled their presence should any Nazi SA troops drop in. If trouble did show up, Auer was counting on the barmaid to discreetly let him know. For weeks, during similar meetings at the pub, he'd made sure to leave her generous tips. If alerted, Auer and his allies had an escape route planned: out the back door and through central Munich's labyrinth of alleys and secluded courtyards.

As the group huddled behind the curtain, they received reports about what was happening on the streets from men with the Social Democrats' paramilitary defense force, the Reichsbanner, who pedaled to the pub on bicycles. Bad as their reports were, worse was coming.

At one point, Auer got up from the table and used a phone in the kitchen to call the Munich Labor House, where the Social Democrats had offices. What he heard over the phone was alarming: The SA was storming the building even as he listened in. A Sturmabteilung unit had set up positions with machine guns in front of the union house, he was told. Then SA men burst inside. Over the phone line, Auer heard shots. As the Reichsbanner defenders filed out of the Munich Labor House, he was told, Bavarian government troops joined the fray, assaulting them with their rifle butts.

A little later, Auer and the others in the pub received further disturbing news: SA men had seized the offices of the *Munich Post*. Wilhelm Hoegner, a leading Social Democratic figure in Munich who wrote anti-Nazi columns for the *Post*, volunteered to walk over to the newspaper office to see what was happening.

Hoegner's route took him past the offices of another anti-Nazi newspaper, *Der gerade Weg*, where SA men were loading bundles of confiscated editions of the newspaper onto trucks and driving them away. Hoegner did not know it at the time, but the editor of *Der gerade Weg*, Fritz Gerlich, was arrested. He was later tortured, and eventually taken to Dachau, the Nazis' first concentration camp, outside of town, where he was murdered.

Hoegner continued walking down Herzogspitalstrasse until he came to Altheimer Eck. "The street was sealed off by a chain of SA men," Hoegner would write in his memoir, *Escaping Hitler*. "A few dozen civilians stood around."

The SA was inside, busy throwing objects out of the broken windows: furniture, typewriters, newspapers, and books, even inkwells. Bedding and pillows were tossed out from the third-floor apartment of the *Post*'s business manager.

"The shadows of the perpetrators darted around the rooms," Hoegner wrote. "But the spectators next to me didn't say a word. The only sound was the dull thumping of objects as they fell to the street."

Hoegner went up to a city police officer who was just standing around.

"Don't you see that private property over there is being plundered and destroyed?" he shouted. "Are the police going to tolerate this?"

"That's not my concern," the officer replied. "I'm not going to get mixed up in that."

At the tavern, Auer still nursed hope that state government troops would put an end to the Nazis' Bavarian coup. Auer had good contacts within the Bavarian Interior Ministry. Those contacts had told him that state police would stand up to the Sturmabteilung and protect Social Democrats. Indeed, Auer felt such an offensive was about to happen when he and his colleagues heard the sound of boots on the street outside, marching in double-time.

"Now there's going to be a clash," Auer said. But the sound of the boots on cobblestones vanished, and there was no clash.

When the SA troops began their raid on the *Munich Post* offices, Edmund Goldschagg happened to be inside. He managed to flee out a back door. That night, he, Auer and others were able to escape immediate capture by going underground, taking refuge at the homes of friends. But in the days and months that followed, as the Nazis tightened their grip on power, the *Post* editors endured cycles of catch-and-release-and-catch-again, intended to terrorize and intimidate them. A knock on the door could come at any moment. They couldn't work and they lived in constant fear.

On the run, Erhard Auer had his beard shaved off so that he wouldn't be as recognizable. And yet he still convened secret meetings with other leading Social Democrats—at his apartment, at the homes of comrades, and at the pub, code-named the "Sea Palace," where they had gathered the night the *Post's* offices were raided.

A glimpse inside those covert meetings was provided by Hoegner in *Escaping Hitler*, written in 1937 but not published until 1977. He also chronicled Auer's sad transformation from a fighter who kept trying to convince himself that all was not lost to a man who finally had to face the truth. Auer and Hoegner were not just socialist comrades; they were also close friends.

To avoid arrest, Auer spent the night of March 10 at the home of another socialist. The next day, he showed up late at a meeting of Social Democratic leaders. He had just learned that SA troopers had stormed into his apartment at 2 o'clock that morning. His family also had spent the night elsewhere, but the maid was there. The storm troopers searched the apartment—throwing books, clothes and other items onto a pile as they looked for any incriminating evidence. When the maid refused to disclose Auer's whereabouts, the Brown Shirts took her away, along with a large cabinet filled with documents.

The SPD leaders heard more bad news: Karl Stützel, Bavaria's interior minister, was kidnapped from his home and dragged off to the basement of the Brown House. Stützel was an upstanding man, a Catholic and member of the Bavarian People's Party (BVP). The conservative BVP was hardly on the same ideological wavelength as Auer and his fellow socialists. But they and Stützel had one thing in common: a loathing of Adolf Hitler. After the Nazi leader's release from prison back in 1924, Stützel banned Hitler from making public speeches and sought to get him sent back to Austria. In 1930, Stützel tried to defang the SA by banning the wearing of their uniform in Bavaria. As the Nazis took over Bavaria starting the night of March 9, it was Stützel whom Auer had hoped would deploy state police to stop them — but by then it was too late.

At their meeting, Auer and the others were told that SS men burst into Stützel's apartment at midnight with pistols drawn. Barefoot and dressed in a nightshirt, the minister was forced into a truck and hauled off to Nazi headquarters. He was later released, badly beaten. He would be no impediment to the Nazis.

Auer, Hoegner and other party associates met again the following evening at the Sea Palace. The horrors just kept piling up. Jewish apartments were being plundered, their inhabitants beaten. Auer's group learned of a rabbi who was taken to a military training ground and made to stand to be shot. When the executioners fired, they intentionally missed the rabbi. The unfortunate man collapsed and was mercilessly beaten.

They heard about the arrests of many local leaders of the Reichsbanner. And they learned that some comrades had fled across the border.

Things got even hotter when, on March 23, 1933, the Reichstag passed the so-called Enabling Act, allowing Hitler to rule by decree, without the consent of the Reichstag. The vote was 444 in favor, 94 against. All 94 were Social Democrats.

It became open season on the leftist party. On his way to one of his covert meetings, just outside the city, Auer was apparently recognized by some Nazi as he got off a streetcar. As the meeting was about to begin, a lookout who had been posted outside burst in to warn that storm troopers were approaching.

"Everyone ran for their coats and then disappeared into every direction," Hoegner wrote in *Escaping Hitler*. Outside, on the darkened street, Hoegner noticed that Auer had not yet come out, and he went back in to get him. "He was a lumbering old man and was unable to run," Hoegner wrote.

As quickly as they could, the two started across a field, stepping in cow dung in the darkness. "In the near distance we heard yelling and engines clattering. Search lights glared," Hoegner wrote. But they were able to walk back into the city undetected.

It was then that Hoegner noticed a change in the old newspaperman and political war horse. As they tried to wipe manure off their shoes on tufts of grass, Auer "complained bitterly about how in a moment of danger each of our friends (at the meeting) thought only of himself, pushing and shoving to get out the door the quickest." Hoegner told Auer he was being unfair.

Auer became increasingly bitter, blaming other Social Democrats, including Hoegner, for the party's collapse. He began to lose interest in keeping up the fight. However, at the same time, Hoegner wrote, Auer nursed hopes that were completely irrational at this point, such as a belief that the ban on the *Post* and other Social Democrat newspapers would be lifted. He even began a legal effort for the return of *Post* printing equipment that had been confiscated — to no avail, of course.

A fascinating episode during one of the Social Democrats' covert Sea Palace meetings bears retelling.

During the Weimar Republic, the Social Democrats had committed themselves not to use violence to bring about political change, unlike the Communists. More than a million people belonged to the Social Democrats' paramilitary self-defense force, the Reichsbanner, but they were banned from having firearms — though some did so secretly.

One night at the Sea Palace, a waitress pushed aside the curtain and whispered to Auer, Hoegner and others that Heinrich

Himmler was drinking red wine in the pub with his deputy, Reinhard Heydrich.

"We peeked through a hole in the curtain, and saw our despised opponents sitting at a table not 20 steps away," Hoegner wrote. Himmler was, of course, the man behind the massive roundups of political prisoners in Bavaria, along with the torture and murders at Dachau.

"We looked at one another and tried to divine what each of us was thinking," Hoegner wrote.

One of the Social Democrats had a pistol. Hoegner doesn't say who, but Auer had carried one for years because of threats he received as a journalist. It would have been so easy, Hoegner wrote, to shoot the two Nazis dead and make an escape.

"There were more than enough reasons for us to do this to Himmler and Heydrich," he wrote. Instead, they quietly returned to the table.

"None of us was a brigand who shot their enemies in the back. We paid up and quietly left the `Sea Palace' through the back door into the courtyard."

It is worth pondering what might have happened had they decided to use the pistol that night. Along with being Bavaria's police chief, Himmler was head of the SS paramilitary organization. He built the SS into a bloodthirsty army that operated the concentration camps that sprang up across Germany and implemented the Nazis' efforts to wipe out all of Europe's Jews.

Would the assassination of Himmler and his deputy in 1933 by a handful of socialists have saved Europe from war and atrocities that were to come? That's impossible to say. But such an act could well have sparked a civil war in Germany, with uncertain outcomes.

Deep political and social fissures in Germany made any meaningful resistance against the Nazis extremely difficult. The Social Democrats had been popular across the country in the years before Hitler rose to power, but support for liberal parties was rapidly eroded by the Nazi leader's growing appeal. Hitler's base consisted of fanatics who were drawn to his use of Jews and Marxists as scapegoats for Germany's problems and were convinced he was the one who could overcome them.

Had the Reichsbanner taken up arms against the Nazis, there would surely have been bloodshed across the land. SA and SS troops would have fought back mercilessly, perhaps with the assistance of civilians supportive of the Nazis. While Hoegner saw the futility in armed resistance against the Nazis in 1933, it was also a source of deep despair.

As he put it in *Escaping Hitler*, "We (Social Democrats) were overwhelmed by the weight of defeat and the feeling of powerlessness, abandoned to our fate, more sad than indignant over the outrages of our enemy . . . helpless, like a herd of cows shivering together beneath trees to get out of a freezing rain."

For a time, Auer had been incredibly lucky, but his luck did not hold. Along with being a member of the Bavarian parliament, he was on the Munich City Council. When, at a May 5 council meeting, he refused to support an ordinance paying tribute to Hitler, Nazis reacted with fury. He was kicked, beaten and dragged out of the council chambers.

Across Germany, the number of Social Democrats, Communists and others arrested by the Nazis was growing so rapidly that new concentration camps had to be built. Just in Bavaria, about 20,000 people had been hauled off by the end of June 1933.

Some chose to kill themselves before the Nazis could get to them. They included Toni Pfülf, a member of the Reichstag from Bavaria who made her mark by championing equal rights for women, especially greater educational opportunities for girls. Depressed by her party's inability to resist the Nazis, Pfülf poisoned herself during the first week of June.

Throngs of Social Democrats—those who had not yet been rounded up or fled the country—turned out for Pfülf's cremation ceremony at Munich's Ostfriedhof cemetery, where the Nazis banned any eulogy. There was a notable absence at the ceremony: Erhard Auer.

He had been arrested again. Released from Stadelheim prison after 10 days, he was tightlipped about his treatment there, but his demeanor made it obvious he had been abused, Hoegner wrote in *Escaping Hitler*. He added, "His rosy confidence never returned after this."

Following his second stint in jail, Auer was banished from Munich by the Nazis. The aging editor moved to Karlsruhe, where he lived under an alias.

Hoegner himself decided staying in Germany was too dangerous. He fled over the Alps into Austria, and then to Switzerland.

Edmund Goldschagg was part of Auer's tight-knit circle and he, too, would have hard decisions to make.

After his getaway on the night of March 9 as storm troopers ransacked the *Munich Post* offices, Goldschagg slept at the homes of friends rather than stay in his apartment on Prinzenstrasse. He sent his wife, Lotte, along with their 3-year-old son to live with Goldschagg's relatives in Freiburg.

A force of political police showed up outside Goldschagg's apartment building one evening in March. "It was a huge presence, with many vehicles with searchlights mounted on their roofs to brightly light up the house and surroundings," according to a 1986 biography of Goldschagg by Hans Dollinger.

"Because Goldschagg wasn't there, they ransacked the apartment, threw his lovingly assembled library of books out the window and hauled their plunder off in a truck," wrote Dollinger.

Goldschagg, who attended some of the secret Sea Palace meetings, was able to escape arrest until June 16, when he spent six nights at the Ettstrassse police lockup in "protective custody," alongside other *Post* editors who were snared in a roundup.

About a week after his release, unemployed and struggling to provide for his family, he joined his wife and son in Freiburg. He no longer dared to chance living underground in Munich.

On June 22, the Nazi regime had issued a fateful declaration. It branded the Social Democratic Party "enemies of the state and of the people."

Gallery Two

People and Places

The parliamentary group of the Deutschnationale Volkspartei (German National People's Party) in the Weimar National Assembly. Front center: Arthur von Posadowsky-Wehner, DNVP parliamentary group President, to his left, Margarete Behm, to his right Anna von Gierke, circa 1919. (Sammlung Berliner Verlag Archiv/picture-alliance/AP Images)

Adolf Hitler, leader of the National Socialist German Workers' Party, October 10, 1923. (AP Photo)

Posing at a rightwing political meeting are Nazi politician and cofounder of Stahlhelm, a German paramilitary veterans organization, Franz Seldte (second from left); Stahlhelm leader Theodor Duesterberg (third from left) and Alfred Hugenberg, businessman and leader of the German National People's Party (fifth from left), October 11, 1931. (AP Photo)

Germany's General Franz Ritter Von Epp, leader of the National Defence Army, in Berlin, Germany, Undated. (AP Photo)

Erhard Auer, chief editor of the *Munich Post*. As a leading official with the Social Democratic Party, Auer was also one of the most influential anti-Nazi politicians in Bavaria. He was arrested and beaten after the Nazi takeover. Circa 1919. (Social Democracy Archive/Friedrich Ebert Foundation)

Martin Gruber, senior editor at the *Munich Post*, made many appearances in German courtrooms to defend the paper against libel lawsuits brought by Hitler and other Nazi officials. The lawsuits were the result of revelations by the paper about Nazi activities. Circa 1921. (Social Democracy Archive/Friedrich Ebert Foundation)

Julius Zerfass, culture editor, was among the *Munich Post*'s top leaders. He was detained after the Nazi takeover of Bavaria in March 1933, sent to the Dachau concentration camp and after his release, relocated to Switzerland in 1934. Circa 1927. (Social Democracy Archive/Friedrich Ebert Foundation)

Edmund Goldschagg, seated, was called up by the German army to serve in World War I in 1914, during which he was wounded, returned to the front lines after recovering and then captured by French troops. After the war, Goldschagg worked as a Berlin-based journalist for the press service of the Social Democratic Party. He became political editor of the *Munich Post* in 1927 and served in that function until Nazi storm troopers violently shut down the paper in March 1933. (Social Democracy Archive/Friedrich Ebert Foundation)

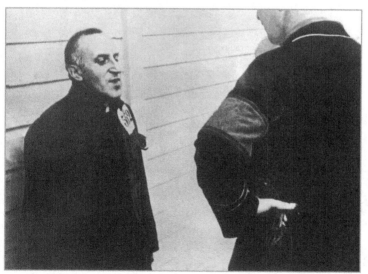

The journalist and writer Carl von Ossietzky as a prisoner in the Sachsenhausen concentration camp, Undated. (Berliner Verlag/Archiv/picture-alliance/AP Images)

The entrance to the infamous Nazi concentration camp at Dachau, Germany, May 3, 1945. (AP Photo)

Prisoners at the electric fence of Dachau concentration camp cheer the Americans in Dachau, Germany, Undated. (AP Photo)

The private home of Adolf Hitler at No. 16 Aussere Prinz Rengenten Strasse, Munich, Germany, May 19, 1945. (AP Photo)

When the Americans took over the occupation of Munich they found 16 bronze caskets containing bodies of men killed during the famous 1923 Putsch, July 20, 1945. (AP Photo)

Dr. Wilhelm Hoegner, the Bavarian minister-president, left, and Rabbi Rosenberg of America talk at a Jewish conference in Munich, Germany, March 1946. (AP Photo/Sanders)

Former *Munich Post* political editor Edmund Goldschagg, right, greets Ernst Langendorf, a U.S. Army officer who in 1945 led a scouting team that searched southern Germany for untainted editors to take leadership roles in newspapers that were being founded under the auspices of Allied occupiers. Goldschagg became chief editor of the Munich-based *Süddeutsche Zeitung*, circa 1947. (Süddeutsche Zeitung Photo)

CHAPTER FOURTEEN

Prisoner No. 2307

Dachau, the Nazis' prototype concentration camp, lay some 20 miles northwest of Munich. After transports of prisoners passed through iron gates that bore the taunting words *Arbeit Macht Frei* (Work Will Set You Free), the abuses began without delay.

As the newly arrived stood in formation, names were called out by an SS guard, holding a folder and "looking like a cattle dealer." Other SS men circled prisoners "like a pack of wolves." A prisoner got a hard slap in the face for wearing a hat with an emblem bearing the colors of the now-murdered Weimar Republic. An SS guard leader had a cigarette dangling from the corner of his mouth, his hands in his trouser pockets, his hat cocked to the side—looking "from head to toe . . . like a pimp wearing a uniform."

Select prisoners were taken into a cellar for interrogation. "The head of the delinquent is wrapped in a wool blanket. An SS beats him interchangeably with a horsewhip and an iron rod, while the others hold him down." Guards shout, "Jewish pig, Commie swine, Marxist pig, Bolshevist dog."

These painful, firsthand descriptions were written by Dachau prisoner No. 2307. His real name was Julius Zerfass.

Zerfass, poet and former cultural editor of the *Munich Post*, wrote about life, misery and death inside the camp in *Dachau: A Chronicle.* The book, published in 1936 under the pseudonym Walter Hornung, reads like a journalist's account of life and death in a concentration camp, because that's precisely what it is. Although it is written in fictional form, Zerfass produced it to show the world the real-life horrors that were happening inside this place where, as he wrote, Jews shot "while attempting to escape" were in fact simply murdered, and where beatings were so vicious that walls dripped with blood. Using fictitious names of prisoners was undoubtedly meant to protect them or their families from even further harm.

In the novel, there is even a prisoner who had worked as an editor for the *Munich Post* —a man who walked with a limp. This is surely Julius Zerfass himself.

The book describes a group of prisoners being marched off to break rock at a gravel pit. Before they start to work, their SS guard barks an order:

"Editors and journalists step forward!"

Four men obey the command.

"That's it?" the SS guard demands. "Anyone from the *Munich Post*?"

"A man with a limp stepped forward," writes Zerfass, who had a lame leg from a gardening accident years earlier.

"No one else?" the SS guard asks.

"No," says the journalist.

"We'll get all of you, you scum," the SS guard snarls.

Picks and shovels are distributed. Some prisoners hack away

at rock, some shovel, others haul gravel in carts. SS guards use their rifle butts on anyone working too slowly, or for any arbitrary reason.

The *Munich Post* journalist is confronted by an SS guard. "Come here," the guard orders. Because of his lame leg, the editor has trouble walking over the mounds of dirt and rock.

"Have you written anything nasty about the Führer?" the guard asks.

"I was never a political editor," the journalist replies.

"But you knew about it, you swine," says the guard, who then kicks the newspaperman in the shin. The editor closes his eyes in pain but says nothing in Zerfass' fictionalized account.

In the nightmare of real life in Nazi Germany, Zerfass was sent to Dachau among a group of Social Democrats on June 30, 1933. Guarded by armed SS men, the prisoners passed through countryside Zerfass knew well. On that journey, Zerfass may have had warm memories of times he and his wife had spent walking and biking in the rural area. Now everything was changed, undone by the upheaval of the last months and years.

Before he was hauled off to Dachau, Zerfass was arrested twice and placed in "protective custody." The first arrest occurred on March 11, just after the Nazi coup in Bavaria. He spent about two months at Munich's Stadelheim prison, along with hundreds of other political prisoners.

Even after his release, the hardships of unemployment, harassment and worry took their toll. In mid-June, eight *Munich Post* staffers, including Zerfass, were so desperate that they went to an arbitration court to file claims to collect their back pay. The judge rejected their claims. A Nazi police officer who was in the room told them, "It's great you are all here together like this. We couldn't have arranged this any better ourselves. So, off you go to the police!"

A truck was waiting outside. The eight were loaded into it and taken to police headquarters on Ettstrasse, where they were crammed into a tiny cell. Also arrested during that sweep were Edmund Goldschagg and veteran *Post* editors Friedrich Göhring, Karl Sortier and Eugen Kirchpfening. The tragic irony of this fraternity behind bars would not have been lost on the sensitive Zerfass. Before the Nazis shut down the *Munich Post*, he, Goldschagg and others were among the newspaper staff who liked to go for a drink with Erhard Auer at the bar of the Hotel Wagner. Joined by other Social Democrats, they'd spend a couple of hours talking and playing cards. Now, following the June 16 arrest, this sorry cadre of *Post* editors spent a week at Ettstrasse before their release.

Just eight days later — about the time when the Nazis' decree labeling Social Democrats as "enemies of the people" was being issued — Zerfass was arrested again. This time, he was sent to Dachau.

At the concentration camp, Zerfass did the work assigned but was always alert, always taking mental notes.

Some verse emerged from this crucible. In a poem included in a collection published just after the war, Zerfass wrote of murders by SS guards:

"Comrade! Once again they killed during the night.
And they tell us it was suicide.
He killed himself,
That's what they claim.
But it was the SS who strung him up.

And then they say, it doesn't matter.
Just remember you could be next."

In that same collection, Zerfass wrote about toiling in the gravel pit:

"The guard barks at us.
The sun is mercilessly hot.
Our hands are torn,
Blood seeps from our wounds.
When will this torture stop?"

Poetry aside, Zerfass' picture of Dachau's cruelties is most viscerally rendered in his novel.

Prisoner No. 2307 meticulously described the camp's operations, including slave labor shops set up there. One shop made furniture for the SS and camp officials. There were also shops where cobblers and tailors worked. Masons made new detention cells and were working on guard towers. One group of prisoners was assigned to build a swimming pool for the SS.

Zerfass' book details the full range of abuses he witnessed at Dachau. Jews and socialists were treated especially harshly. The guards played sadistic games to amuse themselves. In one, an SS guard defecated into a toilet. A prisoner assigned to cleaning latrines was ordered to scoop the excrement out with his hands, put it in a bucket and then wipe it on his face. The SS men then used a hose to wash the excrement off.

"The procedure repeats itself, for as long as it amuses the SS," Zerfass wrote.

In his writings, Zerfass did not go into details about the abuse he personally suffered, other than his mention of the anonymous

Munich Post journalist with a limp in *Dachau: A Chronicle.*

But five months into his confinement, in November 1933, Zerfass's wife, Anna, was allowed to visit him at Dachau. In a letter to Lotte Goldschagg, Edmund Goldschagg's wife, she described the despair she observed in her husband.

"He was frightened and uncommunicative," she wrote. "It was painful for me to see the low spirit he was in when he came through the doors, like he was thinking, 'What do they want with me now?'"

CHAPTER FIFTEEN

Collaborators

The ascension of Adolf Hitler to the chancellor's office in Berlin forced journalists across Germany to do some serious soul-searching. Should they resist? Should they look for some other kind of work? Should they flee Germany?

Most chose to cooperate with the new regime.

The Nazis' seizure of about 200 Social Democratic and some 35 Communist newspapers in early 1933 and the arrests of their editorial staffs certainly served as a warning to all the other newspapers in Germany—numbering about 3,000. But with excitement spreading across the land about the new strongman in Berlin, many newspapers were already predisposed to work with the new masters. Acts of supplication, opportunism and, in many cases, fascist zeal coursed through German news offices in abundance.

On April 30, 1933, delegates at a conference of the Reich German Press Association (RDP) embraced the idea of joining forces with Hitler's expanding communications operations—abandoning Jews and socialists who were among their colleagues.

Reporting on the conference, the association's news organ, *die Deutsche Presse*, said the "tried-and-tested elements" of the press association "and the forward-looking elements of the National Socialist movement have established a link that provides guarantees for successful work on professional matters, but above all on new state policy objectives of the German press."

A substantial majority of the delegates voted for exclusion of "Jews and Marxists" as members.

The RDP's board was tasked with drawing up a new constitution for the organization that would fall into line with a national "Editors Law" to be promulgated by the Hitler regime. That decree, announced by Hitler's cabinet on October 4, gave the power to approve the hiring of journalists to the Nazi state. Wilhelm Weiss, head of the RDP, boasted that "at least 1,300 Jews and Marxist journalists" were fired in 1934, according to *Journalismus im Dritten Reich (Journalism in the Third Reich)*, a 1989 book by Norbert Frei and Johannes Schmitz.

The board of another professional organization, the Association of German Newspaper Publishers (VDZV), also declared its readiness to cooperate with the regime. Chairmanship of the board was taken over by Max Amann, a long-time Hitler toady and chief of the Nazis' publishing company, Eher-Verlag. Six other Nazi publishing chiefs were added to the board.

Eher-Verlag acquired control of newspapers across Germany, and it became one of the largest publishing concerns in the world.

One mechanism employed by the Nazi regime for controlling news was the "Reich Press Conference," choreographed on a daily basis by the Propaganda Ministry in Berlin. At the first news conference, held on March 15, 1933, Josef Goebbels, the freshly appointed propaganda minister, told the gathered journalists: "Of course you will be getting information here. But you'll also be receiving instructions. You should know not only what is happening, but also what the regime thinks about it and how you can suitably make it clear to the people."

Instructions or "suggestions" were regularly given at the Reich Press Conference. Here's a sampling, from *Journalismus im Dritten Reich:*

"The Propaganda Ministry expects that . . . the speech to be given by the Reich Propaganda Minister this evening on the radio will be aired in its entirety." (July 17, 1933)

"A west German newspaper has written polemically about Thomas Mann. This is absolutely unacceptable. Thomas Mann should be erased from the thoughts of all Germans because he is not worthy of being called a German." (January 26, 1937)

"It is acceptable to write positive stories about Greta Garbo." (November 20, 1938)

"A noon newspaper published a report headlined 'Send Jews To Madagascar' with the subheadline: 'Our Viewpoint.' Our [the Nazi regime's] standpoint has only been, that the Jews have to leave Germany. We are indifferent to where they go." (February 28, 1939).

Newspapers fell into line with the new masters' desires with such alacrity that Goebbels himself complained that the press had become monotonous. It's not that Goebbels was looking for challenges to Nazi policy from journalists. But if Germans didn't read newspapers because they were boring, then the Nazis were also losing an important propaganda vehicle.

Some nuances were allowed. This was the case with the *Frankfurter Zeitung,* which had been one of the most influential newspapers during the Weimar era, and one that espoused liberal views. Under the Nazis, the *Frankfurter Zeitung* was used as a showcase to tell the outside world: Look, here's proof that news-gathering in Germany is not being suppressed. While the newspaper's Jewish publisher, Heinrich Simon, was forced out, editors at the *Frankfurter Zeitung* were given more leeway in what the newspaper could say and how it could say it—until the paper folded in 1943.

The *Berliner Tageblatt*, another liberal stalwart of the Weimar Republic, was also given some freedom—but again, only for outside appearances. The *Tageblatt* was shut down in January 1939.

Before the Nazis' rise to power, a number of newspapers had complicated, shifting views about Hitler and authoritarian rule. The largest paper in Munich, the *Münchner Neueste Nachrichten*, spoke out for democratic reforms right after World War I but in the following years occasionally showed sympathy for the radical right—not forgetting the trauma wrought by Munich's failed experiment with Soviet-style government in 1919.

The *Münchner Neueste Nachtrichten* produced some of the most intriguing, conflicted, and tragic German journalists in the years leading up to the Nazi takeover.

Fritz Gerlich and Paul Cossmann, both ultimately victims of the Nazis, were hired by the newspaper as chief editor and publisher, respectively, in 1920. At the same time, Cossmann published the *Süddeutsche Monatshefte*. Bavaria was then governed by Prime Minister Gustav von Kahr, a right-wing politician who tolerated the growth of radical-right parties like the Nazis. Kahr quit in 1921. Two years later, during renewed eruptions of political violence, the Bavarian government appointed him *General-Staatskommissar* (state commissioner general) and gave him virtual dictatorial powers. Gerlich supported Kahr's policies and opposed attempts by the national government to crack down on extreme-right groups, arguing that Berlin should not be meddling in Bavarian affairs.

It wasn't until Hitler's failed 1923 Beer Hall Putsch that Gerlich took a firm stand against the Nazis. He quit the newspaper in 1928 and took a job as a state archivist. While undergoing a spiritual transformation, Gerlich became part owner and editor of an illustrated weekly magazine that he eventually used as a platform to attack National Socialism from a Roman Catholic perspective.

A major industrial conglomerate, the *Gutehoffnungshütte* (GHH) owned a majority stake in the *Münchner Neueste Nachrichten*. Paul Reusch, managing director of the GHH and a bitter critic of the Weimar democracy, tried to steer the newspaper into taking a favorable stand toward Hitler. Like other German industrialists in the late 1920s and early '30s, he courted Hitler in hopes of influencing his economic policies should he come to power.

Reusch had two private meetings with Hitler in 1932: in Berlin on February 23 and in Munich on March 19. Those meetings resulted in an agreement that the *Münchner Neueste Nachrichten* would refrain from "all unwarranted and personal attacks against Hitler and individual National Socialist leaders" during the presidential campaign that was ongoing at the time. Hitler was a candidate but lost in the second round of voting to incumbent President Paul von Hindenburg.

News of Reusch's deal with Hitler came as a total surprise to the paper's editorial managers, who told Reusch he had no right to make such a promise behind their backs. In the face of an editorial uprising, Reusch retreated from trying to enforce the agreement.

In a March 10, 1933 commentary with the headline, "Was that necessary?" editor in chief Fritz Büchner deplored the Nazis' use of force to seize power from Bavaria's state government. Three days later, he and political editor Erwein Freiherr von Aretin were arrested.

The Nazis' takeover of Munich created deep divisions in the *MNN* newsroom. Anton Benz, Büchner's boss, called staff together to discuss what could be done to fend off any Nazi attempts to seize the newspaper. At the same time, a number of his employees showed up at work wearing Nazi insignias. Betz himself was arrested on the night of March 26, and the following week it was Cossmann, the publisher.

Two Nazis were installed to run the newspaper and they quickly fired Jewish employees. Diving into collaboration on Nazi hate propaganda, the *MNN* published anti-Semitic articles produced by a committee that was organizing a boycott of Jewish businesses. Eher-Verlag, the Nazis' publishing company, acquired the *MNN* in 1935. The Nazification of one of Germany's largest newspapers was now complete.

The Nazis seemed to have had multiple motives for treating editors at the *MNN* so harshly. The obvious one was the editors' fight to keep their journalistic independence. There were likely others as well. Aretin and Cossmann were both involved in moves to restore the monarchy in Bavaria, which would have been a direct challenge to Hitler. And the newspaper's extensive reach in southern Germany was certainly an attraction in the minds of Nazi leadership.

Büchner spent about six weeks in jail. He was banished from journalism and from Munich after his release. Betz spent several months in custody. Aretin was taken to Dachau and endured abuse by SS guards until his release in May 1934.

As for Paul Cossmann, he had espoused the Stab In The Back

legend in the mid-1920s, and yet this did nothing to protect him from harm. After his initial arrest, he was freed from jail in 1934. But seven years later the convert to Catholicism was taken to a transit camp for Munich Jews on the outskirts of the Bavarian capital. The 72-year-old editor, who was seriously ill, received a visit from a friend, attorney Josef Müller.

In memoirs written after the war, Müller remarked on the tragic irony that Cossmann, "a man who helped Hitler come to power by propagating the Stab In The Back myth, was now being persecuted by Hitler."

Cossmann told Müller he "deeply regretted that his spreading of this legend had supported Hitler's propaganda." As the two men talked, it became clear that Cossmann viewed his dire situation as "atonement for what he had caused," Müller wrote.

Cossmann was hauled off to the Theresienstadt concentration camp in Nazi-occupied Bohemia. A fellow prisoner recalled that Cossmann would never utter a word bemoaning his fate. He "placed all of his hope on help from the Virgin Mary, whose solicitude would fend off the worst misfortunes," wrote the fellow prisoner, Alois Weiner.

Cossmann died in Theresienstadt of tuberculosis on October 19, 1942. It was 17 years to the day after the start of the Stab In The Back trial.

CHAPTER SIXTEEN

Acts of Defiance

At last, following half a year in Dachau, Julius Zerfass walked out on December 16, 1933. The concentration camp horrors lived on in his mind, and he would wake up screaming in the night. And yet, like other *Munich Post* journalists who'd endured so much, he was not about to bend to the Nazis.

Living on the edge of poverty, Zerfass, his wife and their son moved into a cheap attic apartment in Neuhausen, a Munich borough, and then into a room in an apartment belonging to his wife's brother. Barred by the Nazis from working as a journalist, Zerfass had to search for some other source of income. He tried going door-to-door as a salesman of portable typewriters. After weeks of trying, he had not sold a single one.

A raid by Nazi police was an ever-looming threat. Out of fear that he would be sent back to Dachau, Zerfass sometimes hid inside a garden shed, living like a hermit, with no heat or electricity.

There was only one way to end this daily anxiety about being arrested again and sent back to the concentration camp, where he might face the same tortures and see the killings he had witnessed there—or be murdered himself. Zerfass decided his family must leave Germany.

Nearly a year after his release from Dachau, on November 11, 1934, they fled to Switzerland. The family moved into the small Zürich apartment of another German escapee and an old friend, Wilhelm Hoegner. They received financial assistance from a Swiss charity.

Finally safe and closer to solvent after settling in Zürich, Zerfass urgently took up a new task of resistance and defiance: He began writing his book about Dachau. In a postwar speech about those persecuted by the Nazis, Zerfass said the dead "have the most right to make judgments. Only it is the judgment of silence." With his Dachau book, Zerfass gave voice to the voiceless. He also wrote poems and articles that were published in Swiss newspapers.

Even though Zerfass at first used the pseudonym Walter Hornung while writing in exile, the Nazis were monitoring him. In 1939, he was placed on a list of 47 Hitler opponents to be arrested by the Gestapo if they were seen in Germany. Zerfass was No. 43 on the list—between fellow journalist Theodor Wolff and playwright Carl Zuckmayer.

The entry for Zerfass read: "Before 1933: An editor for the *Munich Post*, belonged to the SPD education committee in Munich, wrote especially venomous articles against the NSDAP. After 1933 Julius Zerfass was in protective custody and subsequently emigrated to Switzerland. Now lives in Zürich and spreads abominable propaganda against the Third Reich."

Edmund Goldschagg performed his own acts of defiance while living in internal exile in his hometown, Freiburg—including one that arguably saved a life.

Officers with the Political Police, a forerunner of the Gestapo, showed up at Goldschagg's home in January 1934 and hauled him off to jail. His offense was a piece of mail he had sent to his wife in Berlin, where she and their son were staying with friends. The envelope contained a newspaper article about marriage, in which the writer said that "only in marriage can a man be a complete man." In the margins of the article, Goldschagg sardonically wrote "Hitler!" and "Röhm!" He was pointing out that neither Hitler nor Ernst Röhm, the SA leader, was married. A postal employee who had snooped through Goldschagg's mail reported him to police, according to Hans Dollinger's 1986 biography of the editor.

Because Lotte Goldschagg was the recipient of the offending piece of mail, she was questioned twice by police in Berlin, an experience that "rattled her nerves," her husband later told friends in a letter quoted by Dollinger.

Edmund Goldschagg faced hours of questioning after his arrest in Freiburg. His name was entered into a register of political criminals, along with his fingerprints, three photographs of himself and other details. Goldschagg's brother, Berthold, tried to win his sibling's release by taking the matter to the state prosecutor in nearby Mannheim. According to Dollinger's book, the prosecutor told Berthold he considered the offense a minor one and he had no objection to releasing Edmund. The editor was once again a free man after four weeks in "protective custody."

Goldschagg, a dapper man with blond hair and a face that looked perpetually optimistic, retained his sense of humor through it all, as shown by his description of his month-long confinement. In a letter to friends, he quipped that in comparison to his detention the previous year in Munich, "the accommodations, meals, etc., were irreproachable."

Still, Goldschagg had to constantly worry that the Nazis would come after him again — perhaps carting him off to a concentration camp instead of to the local lockup. That didn't stop Goldschagg and his brother from discussing politics at family gatherings. While the men differed about some things, they were in total agreement in their opposition to Hitler and their fear that his dictatorship would inevitably lead to war.

Banned by the Nazis from ever working as a journalist again, Goldschagg tried to find other kinds of work in Freiburg. But it was a struggle. Berthold hired Edmund to work in his printing shop as a typesetter in 1936. Even then, earning a living was still difficult because Berthold's printing business had lost customers after the Nazi takeover of Germany. Making matters worse, the Nazis had stripped away Goldschagg's pension, his life insurance and his health insurance.

Goldschagg and his family were surprised in the spring of 1940 when Hitler's Wehrmacht informed the 54-year-old that because he was a reserve officer, he was to be dispatched to serve as commander of an army unit near the French border. His stint did not last long. The fact that Goldschagg had once been political editor of the hated *Munich Post* had escaped the notice of the local military brass. When Goldschagg's superiors were made aware of his background, they called him to Stuttgart and told him that he if wanted to stay in the army, he would have to swear loyalty to Hitler in writing. Goldschagg refused, and he was dismissed from the military.

Goldschagg's rejection of the Nazis would later take a higher form with his help for a woman named Else Rosenfeld.

A middle-aged convert to Judaism, Rosenfeld was facing deportation to a death camp in 1943. She had spent more than a year in an internment camp for Jews outside Munich. She watched in anguish as fellow internees—people she had become friends with, young people, elderly couples—were deported in batches to Nazi-occupied Poland. At the camp, Rosenfeld was a housekeeper, tasked with buying food and other important functions. She did what she could to try to keep internees' spirits up before they were sent to board trains for the east. Her gestures included finding the best china she could for a farewell dinner for deportees.

Rosenfeld eventually learned that Jews were being sent to their deaths. Many internees chose suicide over deportation, and she seriously considered taking that way out as well, she wrote in her 1945 memoir, *I Stood Not Alone*.

As the camp emptied, Rosenfeld herself was placed on the list of deportees. Then, taken off the list because she was needed to keep the camp running, she realized it was just a matter of time before the Nazis decided she was expendable.

Auspiciously, Rosenfeld had friends who knew people involved in smuggling Jews out of Germany. With their assistance, she managed to take a train to Berlin, where she hid out with friends and relatives for a few months, knowing all the while she would not be safe until she left the country. A plan was hatched to sneak her into Switzerland.

Freiburg lies conveniently close to the Swiss border, and Edmund and Lotte Goldschagg were asked if they would be willing to let Rosenfeld stay with them there while awaiting the chance to flee. Despite the deadly danger, they quickly agreed, and she traveled to Freiburg with a forged ID bearing a fake name, "Martha Schröder."

On a late spring day in 1943, Edmund Goldschagg took a

streetcar to Freiburg train station to pick up the woman with graying hair and glasses. In the station's waiting area, they greeted each other familiarly: They had mutual friends in Munich and had previously met during summer vacation. As they boarded the streetcar to take them to the former editor's apartment, Rosenfeld's fear of capture began to melt away. She had implicit trust in Goldschagg, known by his friends and by Rosenfeld's helpers to be a man of courage and dignity.

The new household arrangement proceeded without incident until one day in April 1944, when a police officer asked Goldschagg to come to the station for a private conversation. Goldschagg had no idea what this was about. As it turned out, the police officer wanted to help him, not harass him.

A neighbor of the Goldschaggs had told the officer she had overheard Frau Schröder remarking that Germany would not win the war and something must be done to end it, a statement tantamount to treason. The woman suggested the officer take a closer look at Frau Schröder's past.

While assuring Goldschagg he was certain this was all a misunderstanding, the policeman recommended that Frau Schröder change her residence, just to avoid any future trouble for the Goldschaggs' houseguest.

Clearly, the time had come to try to sneak Else Rosenfeld into Switzerland. Most of the winter's snow had melted by now, lessening the chances that German border guards would spot the tracks while on patrol. The Goldschaggs and their guest said sad goodbyes and wished each other luck. Their son, Rolf, and Else had become close. So that Rolf wouldn't know Else was embarking on a potentially dangerous journey, his parents told him she was taking a temporary job at a children's home in a nearby town.

Under cover of darkness, a helper accompanied Rosenfeld across a hillside near the German-Swiss border. It was April 20, 1944, ironically Hitler's birthday. Rosenfeld could hear a brook rippling below. "Follow the sound of the brook and you will reach Switzerland," the helper told her. Then he left. Continuing on alone, with only the stars for illumination, she suddenly stumbled and fell. Pain shot through her left leg, which she realized was broken.

That's when she heard steps and saw the light of a lantern approaching.

"Please, tell me where I am," she asked the man who was now standing over her.

"Don't worry—you are in Switzerland," said the man, a Swiss border official.

Back in Freiburg, the Goldschaggs knew none of this, had no assurance that their courage had saved their friend. It was not until after the war that they learned Rosenfeld had made a successful escape from Nazi Germany. In a note to a friend, found by Dollinger, Rosenfeld called the Goldschaggs "brave and helpful people who used not just words but also deeds to express their loathing of the National Socialists' criminal methods."

CHAPTER SEVENTEEN

Liberation

On a June day in 1945, a US Army jeep carrying four soldiers rolled across the countryside between Munich and Freiburg. It was about six weeks after Nazi Germany's surrender. The GIs were with a unit assigned to carry out a crucial but difficult mission: find German journalists not tainted by Nazi pasts to hire for the founding of new German newspapers, with American newspapers as the model.

Much of Freiburg was in ruins. When the GIs reached the Bertoldsbrunnen fountain in the center of the city, locals told them how to find their way through the rubble to reach the printing shop owned by Edmund Goldschagg's brother, Berthold. And Berthold told the GIs where to find Edmund. He was working at a local office that distributed food to Freiburg residents.

When Goldschagg heard the Americans' offer of becoming editor in chief of a newspaper to be started up in Munich, he didn't leap at the opportunity. He was reluctant to give up his current job because he felt that he was helping his fellow Freiburg citizens. There were other reasons as well, having to do with what he had gone through while the Nazis were in power.

"I have bad memories of the time in Munich," he told the American scouting team. "The SA raided my newspaper back then and it was difficult for me to wrestle with it." Goldschagg said he needed to discuss the offer with his wife and asked for four weeks to think it over. The Americans said they'd return to hear his decision.

The GI search team had already begun interviewing prospective publishers and editors to launch newspapers in the Americans' southern German occupation zone. Working out of an office on Munich's Renatastrasse, they put together a card-file index of all journalists who had worked in Bavaria. The American military-owned Radio Munich had put out the word that newspaper professionals were being sought. Many prospective candidates were turned down because of their Nazi pasts.

Starting a free press in Munich was of great importance to the Americans. It was here that the Nazi movement had started. Special care was needed to ensure that a reborn news industry could be relied on to foster democracy. Edmund Goldschagg was in the Americans' card-file index. And yet they didn't know whether he was alive until they found him in Freiburg.

In late July, two members of the scouting team returned in their jeep to Freiburg. And they were pleased when Goldschagg told them that his friends, his brother and, above all, his wife had urged him to accept the Americans' offer.

Goldschagg joined two other untainted Germans —August Schwingenstein and Franz Josef Schöningh—in founding the *Süddeutsche Zeitung*. In time, it became one of the most influential and respected newspapers in Germany, and today is read by more than a million people.

The Third Reich had devastated the former staff at the *Munich*

Post, turning them into pariahs who had to struggle to survive. Some died before they were able to enjoy freedom again. Martin Gruber died in 1936 of an illness at age 70. Banned from Munich in 1933, Erhard Auer went into hiding and lived under an assumed name. Also an ailing man, he died at age 70 in Giengen an der Brenz, about 100 miles northwest of Munich.

Goldschagg hired his old friend Eugen Kirchpfening, with whom he'd been imprisoned, to select novels to be serialized in the *Süddeutsche Zeitung*. Wilhelm Lukas Kristl, who had been a *Munich Post* reporter and who went underground to escape arrest, was also able to make a fresh start. Kristl fled to Spain in 1935. He returned to Germany in 1950 and resumed his writing and journalism career, including work for Goldschagg and other Bavarian newspapers.

In March 1983 — on the 50th anniversary of the *Munich Post*'s last day of existence — the *Süddeutsche Zeitung* published an article by Kristl about the late, lamented newspaper. The headline: "A Courageous Newspaper in Hard Times." The subhead read: "Fifty Years Ago: A Violent End of the *Munich Post*." Kristl wrote about the *Post*'s penchant for fighting injustice even before Hitler and about the acts of journalistic courage that led up to its brutal demise. As a journalist who had written for the paper during those proud days, he was just the one to do the retrospective.

So, there were former *Post* editors who died and others who triumphed over the odds. Somewhere in between was Julius Zerfass. He was able to shake off the shackles of Nazism when he fled with his family to Switzerland. But he was never the same. His soul was troubled. Germany was his birthplace, but he felt he no longer belonged there. He was angry that Germans had embraced Hitler and never rose up against him. He watched with bitterness as ex-Nazis returned to prominent positions.

At about the same time that Goldschagg's *Süddeutsche Zeitung* began publishing, Zerfass was offered a job as cultural editor with a newspaper that was being started up in Cologne, the *Rheinische Zeitung*.

"I am in a quandary over what to do," Zerfass wrote in a letter, postmarked from Zürich and dated November 11, 1945. It was addressed to Wilhelm Hoegner, who had since moved back to Munich. "If I returned, I had always envisioned going back to Munich," not some other German city.

"Still," Zerfass wrote, "this is a tempting offer—to have influence on the founding of a significant newspaper." He traveled to Cologne to explore the possibilities, but ultimately he turned down the job offer and returned to Zürich.

Zerfass was eventually able to cobble together something of a livelihood in Switzerland. He wrote for Swiss newspapers, although his activities were restricted until he was able to get a work permit. He also wrote poems and essays that were collected in three volumes after the war. His reflections on his life, on nature, and on his forsaken homeland were captured in this creative work.

When Zerfass sat down to write the poem "To My Heimat," the sweet memories of pre-Hitler Germany that filled his mind were assaulted by remembrances of all that he had suffered en route to his exile. The word "Heimat" means "home." But for Germans, it has deeper connotations. It is a place where you feel you belong, where you feel safe. It is a part of your identity. Zerfass' poem includes these lines:

"Sometimes in my dreams it is to you that I return,
And I feel at home again,
And that I am a part of you—in my dreams . . .
But when I awaken, I am abruptly and harshly made aware,
That the Heimat was only a vision,
Just a painful yearning—in my dreams."

On March 27, 1956, journalists, novelists, poets, and German exiles filed quietly onto the grounds of Zürich Cemetery. They came to pay their respects to one of their own, Julius Zerfass, who had died three days earlier of complications from surgery for stomach cancer. He was 70 years old.

Speakers extolled the journalist-poet for his courage, his humanity, his humility, and his persistence. While so many German intellectuals "bowed to the barbarians . . . let themselves be seduced by barbarism with an ecstatic zeal," Zerfass remained true to his principles, said one speaker. Zerfass, he said, "embodied that other, better, noble, and highly gifted Germany, which was overcome by bestiality."

Said another speaker before Zerfass was cremated: "And thus did Julius Zerfass reach his final day, if not as a victor, then certainly as a warrior."

Fine tributes, but already, the deeds and printed words of the anti-Nazi crusaders of Altheimer Eck 19—Julius Zerfass, Martin Gruber, Erhard Auer, Edmund Goldschagg, and their comrades—were fading into obscurity, like the ghostly wisps of smoke curling from the chimney of the Zürich cemetery crematorium and vanishing into the air.

CHAPTER EIGHTEEN

The Lamb and the Wolf

"We have to look truth in the eye. We must acknowledge the magnitude of the responsibility laid upon us (Germans) by the crimes of the Hitler hordes, and we must not try to push the blame onto others."

The words are those of Julius Zerfass, in an essay titled, "From Vassals to Free Citizens," that was published one year after war's end. The 36-page essay is an astonishingly frank and unforgiving analysis of how Germans came to embrace Hitler — astonishing because dwelling on Germans' culpability for the Third Reich was not welcome in a country that was trying to forget it.

Germans brought shame upon themselves not only by allowing Hitler to rise to power, Zerfass wrote from exile in Switzerland, but also by failing to rise up against him as the Nazi regime mercilessly subjugated other peoples and committed mass atrocities.

"The world," Zerfass wrote, "expected from the (German) people an outburst of wrath . . . and bringing to justice the torturers and executioners who continued their nefarious crimes until the final hours."

Why did Germans not heed repeated warnings about Hitler made by the *Munich Post,* by other newspapers and by political parties that sought to protect the Weimar Republic? Answers to that question are embedded in a larger one: Why did Germans choose to abandon democracy and embrace a despot?

First, it's necessary to review briefly just how Hitler worked the levers of government and the channels of popular anxiety to assume power. In the final two years of the Weimar Republic, Germany was a country of 67 million people reeling from political instability, daily political murders, the Great Depression and from a toxic hatred running deep within the populace. The Social Democrats and other defenders of democracy lost ground to the Nazis and to the Communists. Business leaders, estate owners, middle-class workers, laborers, civil servants, farmers and others yearned for a strong hand. Parliamentary elections of 1930 and 1932 tell the story in stark numbers. A dramatic leap in the number of Reichstag seats won by the Nazis in 1930 — from 12 to 107 — made Hitler's party the second-largest in the national legislature. The Social Democrats remained the largest party but their delegate number dropped from 153 to 143. The Communists increased their delegate count from 54 to 77. Smaller parties shared the remainder of the Reichstag seats.

The seven-year term of President Paul von Hindenburg, a legendary World War I general, was expiring in 1932. Hindenburg decided to run again. He was challenged by Hitler and by Communist Party leader Ernst Thälmann. Hitler aggressively and theatrically wooed voters, making 46 speeches and arriving at his rally locations in a rented airplane — flights called "the Führer Over Germany" in Nazi slogans. Hindenburg won re-election with 53 percent of the vote, but Hitler's 37 percent — more than 13 million ballots — demonstrated that he was to be reckoned with.

Another parliamentary election was held on July 31, 1932, and the Nazis suddenly became the largest party in the Reichstag, their 230 seats far surpassing 133 won by the Social Democrats. The Communists' mandate grew from 77 to 89 delegates. With none of the parties having enough support for a majority, yet another coalition government was formed; there were many during the lifetime of the Weimar Republic. Overtures were made to Hitler to join the government but he spurned them because he wanted the chancellorship and not some lesser role. Chancellor Fritz von Papen, a conservative hostile toward parliamentary democracy, was re-appointed chancellor by Hindenburg. Hitler was the executioner of the Weimar Republic, and Papen was among the politicians who led democracy to the guillotine. Using as a pretext a spike in murders and assaults — many of them from street fights between storm troopers and Communists — Papen deposed the Social Democrat-led government of Prussia on July 20 and placed Germany's largest and most influential state under martial law. Backed by businesses and estate owners, Papen and other major political players had by now consciously set all of Germany on a course toward authoritarian rule.

Yet another Reichstag election was held on November 6, 1932 — the last fully free vote for parliament of the Weimar Republic. Nazi representation in the Reichstag dropped from 230 seats to 196. The Communists gained 11 seats, and their total of 100 put them close to the Social Democrats' 121.

Papen resigned as chancellor and was replaced by the defense minister, Gen. Kurt von Schleicher. But Schleicher's coalition soon fell apart amid meetings between Papen and Hitler about joining forces in a new government. Schleicher resigned and Hindenburg made Hitler chancellor on January 30, 1933. Assumptions by Papen and other conservatives in the cabinet that they would be able to control Hitler soon proved to be delusional.

This brief historical outline explains some of the forces that pulled the Weimar Republic apart. Still, the question remains: Why would Germans choose despotism over democracy? Whatever hardships may be pummeling you and your country, why would you abandon the right to self-government and all of the freedoms that come with it?

Historians have tried to address this question with various theories since the Third Reich's demise. It is a question that Julius Zerfass, in his 1946 essay "From Vassal To Free Citizen," also sought to understand.

The United States, Britain, France, Switzerland and other countries all built successful democracies long before the Weimar Republic, Zerfass points out. He writes about missed opportunities in German history: a 16th century peasant uprising that was bloodily quashed by German princes and landlords; the convening of a National Assembly in Frankfurt in 1848-49 that drew up a proposed constitution that included universal suffrage for men but was rejected by Prussia's king; and the 1871 unification of the German states, establishing an empire known as the Second Reich, that created an elected legislative body called the Reichstag but placed ultimate power in the hands of the Kaiser, his appointed chancellor, the military, and the German princes.

It wasn't until the establishment of the Weimar Republic in 1919 that Germans were given full democratic rights. With a German democracy so long in the making, Zerfass wonders, why were so many so willing to let it go?

He believed part of the answer was to be found at Hitler's rallies, where the Nazi leader —fists clenched and spitting out his words —whipped up anger "to a boiling heat" by using Social Democrats and Jews as scapegoats for Germany's social, political and economic ills. Hitler turned hatred into a powerful political weapon. His proposed solutions for Germany's problems were vague, but that mattered little to the growing number of people who were looking for a political savior.

Hitler knew, wrote Zerfass, that "if one repeats lies often enough, in the end they become the `truth.'"

If Zerfass were alive today, he would surely view the world with alarm. Democratic freedoms —including a free press —are being threatened in many corners of the world, scapegoats are sought, political discourse has turned poisonous, hatred of minorities is growing, extreme-right parties are on the rise.

In his essay, Zerfass wrote that one reason that Germany's first democracy did not succeed was because too many of his countrymen lacked the "will to achieve freedom" —which he also called "political maturity."

"The lamb chose the wolf to be its herdsman," he wrote, using metaphors for Germany and Hitler.

If Zerfass were to write an essay today, he might well amplify his warning, to citizens anywhere who are accustomed to living in a democracy but who see dangers looming. Whatever the threats, whatever the risks, resist, the courageous *Munich Post* editor might say. Remember the perils of allowing rights to wither.

Afterword

Fritz Wagner was born one month before Germany surrendered to the World War II Allies —a "war child," as he calls himself to this day. As Wagner was growing up in Kirn, Julius Zerfass' birthplace, townspeople said little about the Nazis. There was hardly any mention of the Third Reich by his teachers. But Wagner, like many in Germany's postwar generation, wanted to know all about what happened during the Hitler era and what led up to it. "I hated the silence and the hushing-up of events in the years of National Socialism," Wagner recalls. As Wagner expanded his knowledge about the Nazi years, he decided to go into politics. Like Zerfass, Wagner joined the Social Democratic Party.

Just as Germans were trying to forget the Third Reich, Kirn had forgotten about its native son, Julius Zerfass: his boyhood in Kirn, his poetry, his essays, his work at an anti-Nazi newspaper in Munich. It was as if he had never existed. A slim 1982 book, *Ich bin ein Prolet und du ein Prolet* (*I Am A Proletarian, You Are A Proletarian*), by Trier University student Rainer Bohn focused on Zerfass' poetry but also contained biographical details as well as photos of Zerfass. Years earlier, in the 1970s, Hajo Knebel, a local author, wrote about Zerfass for a magazine.

The article caught the attention of a Social Democratic delegate of the Bundestag, Wilhelm Dröscher, known as the "good man from Kirn" because of his personal attention to the concerns and needs of his constituents, and his commitment to just causes. Dröscher contacted Knebel, and the two agreed Zerfass had been overlooked far too long. Knebel tracked down Zerfass' son, Hanspeter, who had in his possession a number of manuscripts written by his father. After Dröscher died in 1977, his family created a foundation to provide financial support for the kinds of causes the "good man from Kirn" had devoted himself to. Rescuing Julius Zerfass from the shadows of history became one of those causes. Knebel began collecting Zerfass' writings with the idea of publishing them in new volumes; he would work with the foundation, with Hanspeter Zerfass, and with Wagner, who became Kirn's mayor in 1982. The first volume, released in 1985, one year before the centenary of Julius Zerfass' birth, was *Daheim und über den Fluss* (*At Home and Across the River*). That was followed over the next four years by three more volumes of poetry and essays and also a reprint of Zerfass' book on Dachau. And again, before those volumes were published, Rainer Bohn was also on Zerfass' trail

"For all of us who were involved in publication of these books," says Wagner, "we wanted honor to be restored" to Julius Zerfass.

Nonetheless, Zerfass remained virtually unknown — as did his colleagues at the *Munich Post* and the newspaper itself.

When I worked as a Germany-based correspondent for The Associated Press from 1987 to '97, I heard there had been an anti-Nazi newspaper in Munich during the Weimar era. While covering 1995 ceremonies marking the 50th anniversary of American troops' liberation of Dachau, I decided to look up an elderly man who I had read in some publication had worked for the *Munich Post*. I found his apartment and he invited me in. He was incoherent as he spoke and struggled with his memory. Frustrated, I left his apartment and never wrote about him. My interest was revived many years later, after the 1998 publication of the best-selling book by Ron Rosenbaum, *Explaining Hitler*. Rosenbaum's book explored the nature of evil and the never-ending quest to understand what it was about *der Führer* that resulted in Hitler becoming the most notorious person in history. A key chapter in Rosenbaum's book is about the *Munich Post*. The title of chapter 3 is "The Poison Kitchen: The Forgotten First Explainers." Using *Munich Post* articles mined from his readings of frail editions of the paper preserved at a Munich library, Rosenbaum was the first author to put a spotlight on the newspaper's tenacious campaigns against the Nazis. Rosenbaum challenged German journalists to build on his work, "to give German readers of today the experience of living through the coming of Hitler through the eyes of Martin Gruber and his heroic colleagues."

I'm an American journalist, not German, but Rosenbaum's appeal resonated strongly with me. During my decade as a correspondent in Germany, much of my reportage had to do with Germany's struggles to come to terms with the Nazi past. When I returned to the U.S. in 1997, Germany continued to haunt me, so much so that I kept researching and writing about German matters in my free time while I was an AP news editor based in Portland, Oregon. I wrote reviews of new books about Germany, travel pieces from Weimar and other places, and about Munich's use of 21st century technology —such as virtual tours of locations linked to the Nazi era —to keep alive the memory of Hitler's victims and of the city's dark past.

I knew that tackling the *Munich Post* would be a big task. Rosenbaum's book had shown me where to find volumes of the newspaper — at a library in Munich. His book also provided the names of the *Post's* key editors, and revealed some of the astonishing articles printed by the newspaper, such as the "Jews In The Third Reich" piece. But a lot of digging lay ahead of me. For a few years, I conducted research by remote. Combing through websites of antiquarian bookshops, I found numerous little-known books that looked like they would be useful: Hans Dollinger's biography of Edmund Goldschagg, Else Rosenfeld's autobiography, a German historian's book on the early years of the Nazi Party, and Douglas Morris' book on Max Hirschberg, the *Munich Post's* attorney. Each volume that was mailed to my Portland home broadened and deepened by understanding of those perilous times. A number of articles published by the *Süddeutsche Zeitung* in decades past also helped me form mental pictures: Wilhelm Kristl's 1983 article marking the 50th anniversary of the SA raid that ended the newspaper's existence, and in 1993 two articles describing in meticulous detail the Nazis' March 9, 1933 coup in Bavaria and the crackdown on Munich's free press.

As intriguing as all of the *Munich Post* editors were, it was Julius Zerfass who for some reason spoke most compellingly to me. I knew vaguely about his humble upbringing in Kirn, that he had trained as a gardener, written poetry, and was one of the last editors for the *Munich Post*. I wanted to know more. It was time for a trip to Kirn.

As I walked into the office of Kirn's mayor one October day in 2009, Fritz Wagner welcomed me with a hearty handshake, a smile, and a bounty of material. Laid out on a table for me were Hajo Knebel's collected volumes of Zerfass essays and poems,

Zerfass' book on Dachau, as well as copies of letters, obituaries of Zerfass that were printed in Swiss newspapers, and other documents I had never seen before. I began reading this material before I flew back to Oregon, and immersed myself in it over the next few months. It did not take long for Julius Zerfass to take up residence in my head. He visited me in my dreams.

Four years later, I traveled to Munich for a month of research. Before I left for Germany, I queried Bavarian State Archives, Munich City Archives, and the Institute of Contemporary History in Munich about what they had on the *Munich Post* and the journalists who worked for it. As stacks of files were handed to me at each of those document-rich and amazingly helpful institutions, I found myself mentally stepping into another dimension: Munich of the Weimar era. Here were court records showing libel cases brought by the Nazis against the *Munich Post*, biographical details on editors, letters written to, by and about them. One day while taking a break from my reading, I walked to the street corner where the *Munich Post* had had its offices. The building with its iconic arched entrance is still there. But I was saddened to see there was no plaque to inform passersby about the historical importance of this building.

There was no greater resource for my work than the *Munich Post* itself. The newspaper chronicled not only this dramatic and often-overlooked era in history but also its own role in those times. Much of my month of research was spent peering through a microfilm reader at a Munich library. The pages of the *Munich Post* have become thin and fragile, much like the skin of a human being of the same age. To protect the precious newspaper volumes, they have been put on microfilm. As I read through hundreds of issues of the *Munich Post* through the microfilm reader, struggling with the ancient Gothic type until I got the hang of it, I began to understand what made its editors tick. They were journalists, yes, but they were far more than that. They were crusaders, defenders of democratic principles that a growing number of Germans at the time were turning their backs on. I was reminded even more forcefully of what I'd felt from the start: Their stories had to be told.

If there are readers who suspect there's some other agenda, some ideological or political point that I wanted to prove with what I have written, I'll make a final comment: There is none. As I've researched this project over the past decade and more, I've done what I've always done as a journalist: gather facts, follow leads, and form a truthful narrative from what I've learned.

Adolf Hitler reading a newspaper in Brown House in Munich, Germany, circa 1931. (AP Photo)

Author Endnotes

Preface.
"The news media landscape . . ." An extensive exploration of German newspapers in the pre-Hitler era is provided by Bernhard Fulda's book *Press and Politics in the Weimar Republic*.

Chapter 1: The Corpse In Hitler's Apartment.
"Martin Gruber wiped . . ." In the *Post*'s detailed reporting on this attack, the newspaper underscored not just the brutality of the assault but the cowardice of the assailants. The two "powerful young men" chose as their victim "the Munich Post's oldest editor, struck him from behind," and then fled, the article said. The tone of the article was intended to sting. Its sarcastic sub headline: "Heroes of The Third Reich."

"Hitler employed . . ." A number of books describe Hitler's use of spectacle during his rallies and election campaigns. One of the best is Richard J. Evans' *The Coming of the Third Reich*.

Chapter 2: The Journalists at Altheimer Eck 19.
"But Zerfass, a modest . . ." The photo mentioned here is in a 1982 book by Trier University student Rainer Bohn, *Ich bin ein Prolet*

und du ein Prolet (*I Am Proletarian and You Are A Proletarian*), which explores Zerfass' place in the tradition of German "worker-poets" and provides details on his life. Zerfass' compatriots described him as a self-effacing man. In a 1911 essay, Zerfass wrote that he was sickly as a newborn and his parents didn't expect him to live. His parents were industrious—they ran a small farm to supplement the father's meager income from his job at the gasworks. But a hard life took its toll. Zerfass' mother died at age 62, and in the 1911 essay Zerfass wrote that she looked like she was 75. But Zerfass had the kind of personality that rose above hardships. It's been said, Zerfass wrote in the 1911 essay, that the "poorest have the greatest defiance to live." He added: "The same is true for me. I . . . treasure this as my best and most important characteristic." It is a strength of character that Zerfass demonstrated throughout his life, even while facing Hitler in a courtroom during a lawsuit trial.

Chapter 3: Hangman Peters.
"As for Hangman Peters . . ." Long after the Nazis' defeat, debates flared up all over Germany over what to do about monuments erected in Peters' honor and streets named after him. Arne Perras' book provides details.

Chapter 4: Before The Fall.
"Before it became . . ." In the 21st century, Schwabing has kept its tradition of being something of a bustling bohemian hub with its popular cafes, bars and restaurants.

Chapter 5: Red Munich.
"On Nov. 17 . . ." David Clay Large, in his book *Where Ghosts Walked: Munich's Road to the Third Reich*, provides a rich and

very readable description of these revolutionary times in the Bavarian capital and how the resulting trauma contributed to Hitler's rise.

Chapter 6: The Stranger from Austria.
"Mayr didn't think much . . ." The "stray dog" quote comes from an article published by *Current History* magazine in 1941 with the title "I Was Hitler's Boss." The article was written anonymously, but it emerged that Mayr was the author. Mayr had joined the Nazi Party but became disillusioned and joined the Social Democratic Party. He fled to Paris in 1933, was later captured by the Gestapo and sent to the Buchenwald concentration camp, where he died in February 1945.

Chapter 7: Hitler Exacts Revenge.
"Hitler's putsch crumbled . . ." Hitler was not one to forget people who had crossed him, including Kahr. In June 1934, Kahr was kidnapped and taken to the Dachau concentration camp, where he was tortured and murdered. Kahr was among the victims of the so-called "Night of The Long Knives," Hitler's wholesale rounding up and killing of enemies and potential threats to his power. The most famous victim in that murder spree, also called the Röhm Purge, was SA leader Ernst Röhm along with his subordinates.

Chapter 8: Stab In The Back.
"Hirschberg called historians . . ." During the trial, Groener revealed that he and Friedrich Ebert, the Weimar Republic's first president, had agreed in November 1919 that the Army would support Ebert's Social Democrat-led government "in return for the new government's suppression of any Bolshevik revolution," according to Morris' book. Groener's testimony

bolstered arguments that the 1918 upheavals that overthrew the Kaiser resulted from military losses and were not the cause of Germany's defeat, according to Morris.

Chapter 9: Return Of The Brown Menace.

"Earlier that month . . ." The murder of Herbert Hentsch, especially the grisly way it was carried out, revolted people across Germany and not just readers of the *Munich Post*. Some newspapers published photos of Hentsch's corpse, tied up inside the sack just after it was fished out of the water.

Chapter 10: "The Solution Of The Jewish Question".

"The Nazi doctors . . ." Gregor Strasser, who participated in the 1923 Beer Hall Putsch, helped build the Nazi Party, but disagreements with Hitler over political strategy cost him his life. He was among those murdered during the summer of 1934 Röhm Purge.

Chapter 11: Vermin In The Brown House.

"The *Post* was undeterred . . ." Of the intended victims of this plot, ultimately only one survived the vicious power struggles that occurred among Hitler's subordinates Along with Ernst Röhm, Spreti-Weilbach and Uhl were murdered during the 1934 Röhm Purge. Georg Bell, who fled to Austria after Hitler came to power, was assassinated by Nazi commandos in his hotel room in April 1933. Du Moulin-Eckart was arrested during the 1934 Röhm Purge but his life was spared. He was held in concentration camps until 1936. He died in 1991.

Chapter 12: Democracy Dismembered.

"Theodor Wolff . . ." Citations of German newspapers' reactions to Hitler's appointment as chancellor come from Norbert Frei's and Johannes Schmitz' highly informative book, *Journalismus im Dritten Reich* (*Journalism in the Third Reich*).

Chapter 13: "Enemies of the State and of the People".
"The SPD leaders heard . . ." After Stützel was released from jail he briefly fled Germany but returned to be with his family. Watched by the Gestapo, he was considered *persona non grata* in Munich. He died in July 1944 at age 72. In 2017, a Munich square was named after Stützel to recognize his opposition to Hitler.

Chapter 14: Prisoner No. 2307.
"Dachau, the Nazis' . . ." The Dachau camp, built on the grounds of an abandoned munitions factory, opened on March 22, 1933 as the Nazis' first mass incarceration site for political prisoners. The first prisoners were Social Democrats, Communists and trade unionists from Bavaria. Dachau became a model for other Nazi concentration camps, and was used as a training center for SS guards. The camp's prisoners were liberated by American troops on April 29, 1945.

Chapter 15: Collaborators.
"On April 30, 1933 . . ." Descriptions of the Nazi regime's ease in taking control of German new media come from Norbert Frei's and Johannes Schmitz' *Journalismus im Dritten Reich*.

Chapter 16: Acts of Defiance.
"At last, following half . . ." Zerfass' post-Dachau life is described in sometimes heartbreaking detail by his son, Hanspeter, in a letter printed on the last 27 pages of *Schrift des Lebens* (*On Life*), one of the volumes of collected essays and poems by Julius Zerfass published by the city of Kirn starting in 1985.

Chapter 17: Liberation.
"On a June day . . ." Descriptions of American troops' search for untainted German editors and their talks with Edmund Goldschagg come from Hans Dollinger's biography of the newspaperman.

Selected Bibliography

Behrend-Rosenfeld, Else R. *Ich stand nicht allein.* Munich: C.H. Beck'sche Verlagsbuchhandlung, 1988

Dollinger, Hans. *Edmund Goldschagg.* Munich: Süddeutscher Verlag, 1986

Evans, Richard J. *The Coming of the Third Reich.* New York: The Penguin Press, 2004

Frei, Norbert and Schmitz, Johannes. *Journalismus im Dritten Reich.* Munich: C.H. Beck'sche Verlagsbuchhandlung, 1989

Fulda, Bernhard. *Press and Politics in the Weimar Republic.* Oxford: Oxford University Press, 2009

Heiden, Konrad. *Der Fuehrer.* London: Robinson Publishing Ltd, 1944

Hoegner, Wilhelm. *Flucht vor Hitler.* Frankfurt am Main: Fischer Taschenbuch Verlag, 1979

Hornung, Walter (Julius Zerfass). *Dachau: Eine Chronik.* Zürich: Europa-Verlag, 1936

Hoser, Paul. *Die politischen, wirtschaftlichen und sozialen Hintergründe der Münchner Tagespresse zwischen 1914 und 1934: Methoden der Pressebeeinflussung.* Frankfurt am Main: Peter Lang Verlag, 1990

Knebel, Hajo, ed. *Aus grosser Zeit 1933-1945. (From The So-Called Time of Greatness 1933-1945).* A collection of essays and poems by Julius Zerfass. Kirn, Germany: Stadt Kirn, 1986

Knebel, Hajo, ed. *Schrift des Lebens (On Life).* A collection of essays and poems by Julius Zerfass. Kirn, Germany: Stadt Kirn, 1989

Knebel, Hajo, ed. *Daheim und über den Fluss (At Home and Across The River).* A collection of essays and poems by Julius Zerfass. Kirn, Germany: Stadt Kirn, 1985

Langer, Peter. "Paul Reusch und die Gleichschaltung der 'Münchner Neuesten Nachrichten' 1933." Vierteljahrshefte für Zeitgeschichte, 2005. pp 203-240

Large, David Clay. *Where Ghosts Walked: Munich's Road to the Third Reich.* New York: W.W. Norton & Company, Inc., 1997

Ludecke, Kurt G.W. *I Knew Hitler.* Barnsley, Great Britain: Pen & Sword Books Ltd, 2013

Maser, Werner. *Adolf Hitler: Legende — Mythos — Wirklichkeit.* Munich: Bechtle Verlag, 1971

Maser, Werner. *Die Frühgeschichte der NSDAP.* Frankfurt am Main: Athenäum Verlag, 1965

Morris, Douglas G. *Justice Imperiled.* Ann Arbor, Mich.: The University of Michigan Press, 2005

Pridham, Geoffrey. *Hitler's Rise to Power.* New York: Harper Torchbook, 1974

Rosenbaum, Ron. *Explaining Hitler.* New York: Harper Perennial, 1999

Weitz, Eric D. *Weimar Germany.* Princeton, N.J.: Princeton University Press, 2007

Acknowledgments

One fall day in 1972, on the campus of a small liberal-arts college in Vermont, a pretty student with long dark hair sat beneath a maple tree with an open book on her lap. I gathered my courage and approached 19-year-old Christina Peterson. The book was a novel by Thomas Hardy. She spoke of her love for literature. I was studying history at the college and wasn't much of a fiction reader then, but I resolved to become one. We spent more and more time together — canoeing on a quiet lake, walking in the woods, watching the sunset over the Adirondack Mountains from a Vermont hilltop. Friendship became love. We married in 1980, and have been together ever since. This book could not have happened without Chris. I was insecure before we met. She brought me out of my shell, gave me confidence. Her strength of character, wisdom and love steered us through huge changes over the coming years — moving from place to place as I took new jobs, our decade living in Germany, readjusting to American culture when we returned. Chris gave birth to our son, Tristan, in 1985, two years before we moved overseas. As I pursued my career in journalism, Chris made personal sacrifices to make sure that our son got the love, care and upbringing that he deserved.

Because of her fortitude and forbearance, our family rose above the trials and tribulations that come with a high-stress job like journalism. I would be nothing without her. Thank you, my best friend, my dear heart.

I am also indebted to retired history professor Elizabeth Sumner. One year before I spotted my future wife reading Thomas Hardy on the campus of Castleton State College, when I was in my sophomore year there, I chose history as my major. Beth Sumner was my advisor and favorite teacher. An expert on the French Revolution, Beth brought history to life and showed me the joys of digging into the past. I transferred from Castleton to the University of Vermont in Burlington, where I narrowed my primary interest in history to Germany. Over the nearly five decades that have followed, Beth has always been a lodestar. We stayed in touch as my career in journalism developed. Whenever I visited family in Vermont, I would stop in to see Beth at her charming old home in Hubbardton. We would talk for hours about politics and history. Books, documents and copies of The New York Times and The New York Review of Books were strewn around the house. I felt right at home. A fire crackled in the fireplace. And when I left her house, my mind would be abuzz with ideas. Thank you, dear Beth.

I'm grateful to a third strong woman in my life: my mom, Kay Petty. When I graduated from high school in Fair Haven, Vermont, in 1969, I had no idea what I wanted to do with my life. It was my mom who intuited that college was best for me. Thank you, Mom.

As I researched and wrote this book, I sensed a presence watching over my shoulder. He was invisible, but he couldn't hide his identity: the late author Peter Wyden. I met Peter at a posh Berlin hotel in the 1990s. He was among German-born

Jews who were taking part in a reunion of people who attended a school for Jewish children. Wyden fled Germany with his family in 1937. I interviewed Peter for an AP story, and he introduced me to some of his former classmates. Peter and I became instant pals. He was larger than life, with a big smile and a roaring laugh. I'd call his home in Connecticut occasionally to pick his brain about possible stories on Germany. Peter was a consummate digger. He loved nothing more than going through documents and interviewing people. His skills produced acclaimed books like *Bay of Pigs*, *Stella* and *Wall*. Peter died in 1998. But his passion for research left a lasting impression on me. I knew that, as I worked on this book, he would have approved.

There are also numerous people and institutions in Germany whose encouragement and support helped make this book possible. They include Dr. Bernhard Grau, director of the Bavarian State Archives; staff at the Munich City Archives; the Institute for Contemporary History in Munich; Christian Ude, a Social Democrat and former mayor of Munich; and Ulrich Meyer, a former journalist who later became a press spokesperson for the Social Democratic Party in Bavaria. The Friedrich Ebert Stiftung, a nonprofit political foundation associated with the Social Democrats, was very helpful in our search for photos of the *Munich Post*'s editors.

A special thanks to American journalist Ron Rosenbaum for his pioneering work on the *Munich Post*.

And my gratitude to Peter Costanzo, AP's digital publishing specialist who championed this book and Mimi Polk Gitlin of Gaia Entertainment. Their wisdom and guidance brought my years of work on this project off my computer's hard drive and into the public arena.

Enemy of the People

The editor of this book, Chris Sullivan, deserves special thanks. A fellow AP retiree, Chris spotted the strengths and weaknesses of my initial draft. Our conversations during the editing process inspired me to take another look at documents and books I had used for research, and at articles printed in the *Munich Post*. This brought greater richness to my book and breathed life into the personalities, especially the editors of the *Munich Post*.

About the Author

Credit: Tristan A. Petty

Terrence Petty was an Associated Press journalist for thirty-five years. Retired since 2017, he was based in Bonn from 1987 to 1997, where he covered German and European affairs, traveling between West and East Germany during the Cold War. During the late 1980s and 1990s, from the pro-democracy movement and reunification to neo-Nazi violence and the fiftieth-anniversary ceremonies at Dachau and Buchenwald, he filed extensively from the country. From 1999 to 2017 he managed the AP's news operation in Oregon. Before joining the AP, Petty worked for newspapers in Vermont and upstate New York. Raised in Fair Haven, Vermont, he graduated from the University of Vermont in 1974 with a BA in history. Petty and his wife, Christina, live in Portland with their son, Tristan.

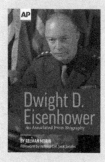

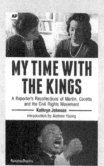

Made in the USA
Coppell, TX
02 September 2020

35927235R00089